First Edition

An Introduction to Programming and Software Development using Java

Eric C. McCreath

School of Computer Science

The Australian National University

1

Forward

Although, there are many good introductory text books on programming in Java, the reason for writing yet another one was to provide one that exactly matched the first year subject that I teach at ANU. Also I wanted to create a textbook that was "free" to students and others. This project started at the end of 2008 and originally I made used of a `Wiki' and enabled students to freely edit this document, however, after a year without any edits from students (at least any that I noticed) I thought it best I just move it to a normal text book format. Any ideas on how this material could be improved are more than welcome.

I am happy for other lecturers to make use of this text for teaching their programming courses. This includes having it printed as part of course notes. Note the Creative Commons ShareAlike licence below.

Eric McCreath 23/4/2010

Table of Contents

1. Introduction

Programming is a creative art. Programming involves a number of stages:

- understanding the problem and the problem domain you wish to solve,

- working out a plan that will solve the problem,

- implementing this solution in the context of a particular programming language and environment,

- testing your solution for correctness, and

- installing/maintaining your program.

Many different approaches can be taken for solving particular problems. The processes involved can be at times challenging and frustrating, yet the process can be also stimulating and provide a great sense of achievement as you produce a complex useful artefact.

1.1. Hello World - Your First Java Program

Below is some Java code for a simple program that prints "Hello World!" to the standard output. When you run this program from the command line you will see "Hello World!" appear on the next line. This is often the first program computer programmers will write when they use a new language. Such a program reveals a little bit about the syntax and semantics of the language. Also by writing and executing such a program the programmer gains some experience in the development environment. I would strongly encourage students to have a go at doing this.

```
public class Hello {
    public static void main(String[] args) {
        System.out.println("Hello World!");
    }
}
```

1.2. Compiling and Running Java Programs

To compile and run programs in Java you require a Java SDK (Software Development Kit) these are generally installed on student lab systems. However it is also possible to install and use one from your home computer or laptop. The two main programs that you use in the SDK are: 'javac' which compiles the Java source code into Java byte code; and 'java' which starts a Java virtual machine and runs your byte code.

Generally each class is stored in a separated text file. These files are named using '<class name>.java' where the <class name> is the same as the class name stated within the file (the Hello class above would have the file name Hello.java). Once compiled the byte code is stored in a file called '<class name>.class' (Hello.class in the Hello class example). To compile and run Hello.java from a terminal one would type:

```
% javac Hello.java
% java Hello
Hello World!
```

A short demo of creating and running a simple hello world program using the command line and text editor is available at :
http://cs.anu.edu.au/people/Eric.McCreath/aipsdj/HelloWorldTerminal.ogg (~23M)

1.3. Eclipse

Eclipse is a very powerful tool for developing software. Eclipse has a large number of features that helps in development of the most complex programs, however, it is still a very useful tool even if you only learn and use a small subset of these features. The main aspects you will need to learning are: creating/managing projects, creating/editing classes, and running your programs. A lot of this is best learnt by demonstration and experimentation. When you run into problems ask someone (colleague, tutor, forum, google, or lecturer).

To get people started there is a video of creating a Hello World program in eclipse: http://cs.anu.edu.au/people/Eric.McCreath/aipsdj/HelloWorldEclipse.ogg (~10M). The 10 features I like about Eclipse are: project/class management, import organizing, method completion, error underlining, stack trace line locater, renaming methods/classes, formatting code, tracking down the code for external classes, debugger, and JUnit testing. I have created a short video on these: http://cs.anu.edu.au/people/Eric.McCreath/aipsdj/10ThingsEclipse.ogg (~109M some lag between sound and vision).

2. Basic Data Types

Information is stored within a computer using a variety of different standard basic data types. At one level the computer's storage is just a very large collection of bits (ones and zeros). The hardware groups these bits into lots of 8, these are called bytes. Memory or data files are normally addressable at the byte level. Programs and users interpret these bytes to be of a particular data type. The the basic data types in Java include: integers, booleans, doubles, and characters. The format of these are defined at the bit level.

Suppose a particular location in main memory contained the following bits:

```
01100100011011110110011101110011
```

This would be broken up into 4 bytes:

```
01100100, 01101111, 01100111, 01110011
```

If a program interpreted these 4 bytes as an integer then it would be the number:

```
1685022579
```

Whereas, if a program interpreted the 4 bytes as a floating point number then it would be the number:

```
1.7664905E22
```

A program could also interpret the 4 bytes as the characters that make up the string "Dogs".

Java helps us as programmers to interpret data in memory. In Java we label the data as a particular data type and Java restricts us to use methods and operators that make sense of a particular data type.

In a block of code in Java we can set aside some memory for storing a basic data type. This memory can be referred to by name, these names are called variables. To declare a variable in Java we give the type of the variable, its name, and a semi-colon. Suppose we set aside some memory for an integer which we call "age". The block of code in Java would be:

```
int age;
```

Once the variable is declare we can assign it to a particular value (write data into the memory location). The assignment operator is used to set a variable to a particular value.

```
age = 21;
```

As a program will often declare a variable and immediately assign it to an initial value, Java lets you do both in one line. e.g.

```
int age = 21;
```

We can also read the current value of a variable just by referring to its name in an expression.

```
int year = 2009;
```

7

```
int birthYear = 1970;
int age;
age = year - birthYear;
```

Often we will declare a number variables of the same type at the same time. This can be done by listing variable names with comma separation. e.g.

```
int width, length, height;
```

A variable may only be used after it is declared and within the block of code it is declared. This is know as the variable's scope. Outside of this scope the variable may not be used. In fact outside the scope the variable may not even exist!

2.1. Integer

The integer basic data type provides a way of representing whole numbers that range from –2147483648 to 2147483647. Java uses 32 bits or 4 bytes to store these numbers. The keyword 'int' is used to declare an integer. Integers are a key data type for programmers and they are used in a multitude of situations including: counting a number of items, indexing into arrays or lists, referring to the length of an array, storing integer type data, etc. Always remember the integer has a limited range, so you must be certain that your program will not run over either end.

The operators you most often use on integers are :

Operator	Name	Description	Example	Example's Result
+	Addition	adds two integers	2 + 3	5
-	Subtraction	subtracts the second integer from the first	5 - 7	-2
*	Multiplication	multiply two integers	2 * 3	6
/	Division	The first number is divided by the second(the fractional part is ignored). (more examples)	10 / 3	3
%	Modulo	The remainder when the first number is divided by the second. (more examples)	10 % 3	1

Basic Example of Using Integers

```
// Integer Example Code
// Eric McCreath 2008

public class IntegerExample {
        public static void main(String[] args) {
                System.out.println("Addition 2 + 3 = " + (2 + 3));
                System.out.println("Subtraction 5 - 7 = " + (5 - 7));
                System.out.println("Multiplication 2 * 3 = " + (2 *
3));
                System.out.println("Division 10 / 3 = " + (10 / 3));
                System.out.println("Modulo 10 % 3 = " + (10 % 3));
        }
}
```

8

Java uses the 2's complement representation for storing integers. This representation is generally hidden from the programmer, however, from time to time a programmer will need to understand the bit level representation of integers. Note this representation is the same on all Java virtual machines. Java provides a number of operators that enables you to manipulate integers at the bit level. These operators include 'bitwise and', 'bitwise or', 'bitwise negation', 'shift left', and 'shift right'.

Operator	Name	Description	Example	Example's Result[1]
&	bitwise and	and's corresponding bits in two integers	9 & 10	8
|	bitwise or	or's corresponding bits in two integers	9 | 10	12
~	bitwise complement	each bit in the integer is flipped	~ -2	1
a << b	left shift	shift all the bits in 'a' to the left by 'b' places (0's are added from the right)	9 << 2	36
a >> b	right shift	shift all the bits in 'a' to the right by 'b' places (the value of the left most bit is duplicated and added from the left)	9 >> 2	2

2.2. Boolean

Booleans provide a way of representing information that is either true or false. The keywords 'true' and 'false' are used for stating the boolean literals. There are a number of standard operations that can be performed on booleans. These are:

Operator	Name	Description	Example	Example's Result
a & b	and	does a logical 'and' on 'a' and 'b'	true & false	false
a | b	or	does a logical 'or' on 'a' and 'b'. Note with this operator if both are true then the result is true.	true | false	true
a ^ b	xor	does a logical 'xor' on 'a' and 'b'. Note with this operator if both are true then the result is false.	true ^ false	true
!	logical complement	false becomes true, and true becomes false	! true	false
a && b	conditional and	logically the same as &, but 'b' is only evaluated when 'a' is true.	true && false	false
a || b	conditional or	logically the same as |, but 'b' is only evaluated when 'a' is false.	true || false	true

---

1 You will need to look at the bit pattern of these integers to understand the examples.

2.3. Double

The 'double' provides a way of approximating real numbers within your program. So for example if you wished to store the height of a person then you could use a double.

```
double height = 1.86;  // in meters
```

The literals may also contain exponent terms. e.g. 3.6E-3 is the same as 0.0036. Doubles use 64 bits for storing the number. Note that, generally only an approximation to a particular number is stored. This approximation can create rounding problems. So for example if you were representing 1.86 with a limited number of decimal places (say one!) then your closest representation would be 1.9. Now if you multiplied this number by 2 you would end up with 3.8 even though 3.7 would be closer to 2 times 1.86. In Java double also only has a limited number of 'binary' places to represent a number and it suffers from a similar rounding problem. When numbers are printed, Java will round the number to the closest decimal representation, so you generally do not notice these rounding problems.

The operators you most often use on doubles are :

Operator	Name	Description	Example	Example's Result
+	Addition	adds two doubles	2.1 + 3.2	5.3
-	Subtraction	subtracts the second double from the first	5.0 - 7.0	-2.0
*	Multiplication	multiply two doubles	2.0 * 3.0	6.0
/	Division	The first number is divided by the second.	10.0 / 3.0	3.3333333333333335

Also the Math class provides a number of very useful methods that operate on doubles. These include:

Method Signature/Constant	Description	Example
Math.PI	A double approximation of PI	area = Math.PI * r * r;
public static double floor(double a)	Finds the largest whole number that is less than or equal to 'a'	System.out.println(Math.floor(3.9)); // prints 3.0
public static double ceil(double a)	Finds the smallest whole number that is greater than or equal to 'a'	System.out.println(Math.ceil(3.9)); // prints 4.0
public static double round(double a)	Rounds 'a'	System.out.println(Math.round(3.9)); // prints 4.0
public static double pow(double a, double b)	takes 'a' to the power of 'b'	System.out.println(Math.pow(2.0,3.0)); // prints 8.0
public static double abs(double a)	calculates the absolute value of a	System.out.println(Math.abs(-3.9)); // prints 3.9

The formatter within the String class can be used to format doubles when they are converted into strings for printing. This is illustrated with the below examples:

```
System.out.println(String.format("%.3f",31.9)); // (use floating format and 3 decimal places) prints 31.900
System.out.println(String.format("%.4e",31.9)); // (use exponent format and 4 decimal places) prints 3.1900e+01
```

2.4. Character

The 'char' primitive data type enables you to represent a single character. The literals are give by including the single character between single quotes. Below is some examples of assigning some characters:

```
char letter1 = 'a';
char letter2 = 'B';
char newLineChar = '\n';
```

Characters occupy 16 bits so they range from '\u0000' to '\uffff' or from 0 to 65535.

The Character class provides a number of useful methods to operate on characters. e.g. toLower, toUpper, isDigit, ...

2.5. String

Strings provide a way of representing a sequence of characters. So suppose you wish to store a person's name then you could use a String.

```
String name = "John Smith";
```

The '+' operator enables you to concatenate strings together to form new strings.

```
String firstName = "Kevin";
String lastName = "Rudd";
String fullName = firstName + " " + lastName;
```

Two import things to remember about strings is that they are reference types and they are immutable. Being a reference type, Java handles strings within a program by using a `reference' to the string. A reference is like a pointer to another location of memory. So in the below example there is two strings constructed, initially str1 and str2 are a reference to "Hello" however the final assignment statement changes the reference str1 to "World".

```
String str1 = "Hello";
String str2 = str1;
String str3 = "World";
str1 = str3;
```

The figure below illustrates the above code:

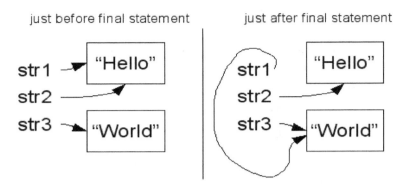

Once a string is constructed it never changes (strings are immutable). So if you wish to modify a string then you must create a new string with the modification and then move the reference to the new string. Say we wish to add "s" to string "World" then we could do:

```
String str1 = "World";
str1 = str1 + "s";
```

The figure below illustrates the above code. The "World" string remains in the program although it is useless as nothing can get hold of it. Every so often the "garbage collector" will remove objects, like the "World" string, that have nothing referencing them.

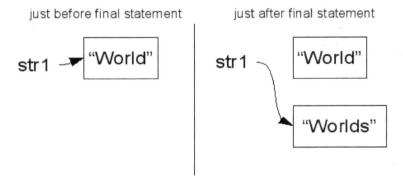

When comparing two strings one should always use the **equals** method. This is because '==' will only check if the references are the same it will not check if the content of the string is the same. Whereas the **equals** method will check if the content of the strings are the same. Note that, if the reference is the same then the content will also be the same, however, the references could be different yet the content could be identical!

Some useful methods that you can use on strings include:

Method	Description	Example Expression (assume str = "Hello")	Example's Result
int size()	determine the number of characters in the string	str.size()	5
char charAt(int index)	returns the character at a particular index	str.charAt(1)	e

2.6. Expressions and the Assignment Operator

Expression are recursive structures which when evaluated return a value. e.g. if the variable "x" contained the value 7 then the expression "x + 4" would obtain the current value of "x", namely 7, and add 4 to it and return 11. Expressions will return a value of a particular type. e.g. the expression "3.5 * 7.8" would return a double. Expressions may involve: literals, variables, fields, operators, and methods. Expressions can be used within parameters of a method call. So in the example below the expression for calculating the parameter for the 'println' method involves concatenating a number of strings together. Note the expression is evaluated before the 'println' method is called, only a single completed string is passed to the 'println' method.

```
System.out.println("Name : " + name + " Age : " + age);
```

The assignment operator, namely "=", is used to set the value of a variable or a field. The variable (or field) is put on the left hand side of the operator and an express is paced on the right hand side. A few examples of using the assignment operator in a statement are given below:

```
x = 6;
y = x + 4;
str = "x : " + x;
lenPlus4 = str.size() + 4;
```

Note the assignment "=" may be used in an expression as it also returns the value that has been assigned. This is not used that often but is worth knowing about. Some examples are below:

```
System.out.println("x : " + (x = 5));
  // set x to 5 and print out  the string "x : 5"
x = (y = 4);
  // set y to 4, "y=4" returns the value 4 which is used to set x to 4
i = j = 0;
  // set j to 0,  "j = 0" returns 0 which is used to set i to 0 also
```

The conditional expression enables you to evaluate and return one expression if a condition evaluates to true otherwise a different expression is evaluated and returned. The expression has the following syntax : "(condition ? exp1 : exp2)". When such a conditional expression is evaluated the "condition" is evaluated first, if the "condition" evaluates to true then "exp1" is evaluated and returned; otherwise "exp2" is evaluated and returned. This can at times be very useful as it can often lead to shorter and more compact code. An example is given below:

```
System.out.println( hats + " hat"  + (hats > 1 ? "s" : ""));
```

2.7. Arrays

Arrays are a basic data type within Java. Arrays store a fixed length list of items of the same type. Items in the array are indexed from 0 to n-1, where n is the number of elements of the array.

Below is an example of using an array to store a list of your friends names:

```
String friends[] = new String[3];
friends[0] = "Bill";
friends[1] = "Jill";
friends[2] = "Phil";
```

You could also create and initialize the array in one line.

```
String friends[] = {"Bill", "Jill", "Phil"};
```

You can look up an element within the array (be careful to keep the index within the defined range):

```
System.out.println("My second friend : " + friends[1]);
        // would print "My second friend : Jill"
```

You can also set elements of an array:

```
friends[2] = "Milly";
        //  The array would now contain  {"Bill", "Jill", "Milly"}
```

The keyword 'length' can be used to determine the fixed length of an array. So the expression:

```
friends.length
```

would evaluate to 3.

Once the length of an array is set at creation it can never be changed. So in the above example you could not add any more friends to your list of friends. (Also removing a friend would cause difficulties as you could blank a name out but the length of the list would remain 3.)

2.8. Additional Material

Integer Division Examples

Expression	Result	Comment
12 / 3	4	
13 / 3	4	Note how the remainder is ignored.
14 / 3	4	
15 / 3	5	
-13 / 3	-4	Take care with integer division with negative numbers (often not used).
13 / -3	-4	
-13 / -3	4	
12 / 0	ArithmeticException : / by zero	If you are dividing by zero then there is a problem in your code.

Integer Modulo Examples

Expression	Result	Comment
12 % 3	0	
13 % 3	1	
14 % 3	2	
15 % 3	0	
-13 % 3	-1	Take care with integer modulo with negative numbers (often not used).
13 % -3	1	
-13 % -3	-1	
12 % 0	ArithmeticException : / by zero	If you are dividing by zero then there is a problem in your code.

The nice thing about the way negatives are done is that the following equality holds for both negative and positive numbers: x == (y * (x/y) + (x%y))

3. Methods and Flow Control

3.1. Basics

Code in Java will execute sequentially - statement by statement. However, you often wish execute the same (or similar) code a number of times, rather, than cut and paste the code a number of times the code may be grouped into a method. Then the new method may be called a number of times. This has a number of benefits such as: simplifying code, shortening code, reducing the chance of error, and it also makes code easier to modify. We now look at an example to demonstrate this idea.

Below is some code that prints a number of people's names and ages in a list:

```java
public class NamesList {
        public static void main(String[] args) {
                System.out.print(String.format("%-8s", "Eric"));
                System.out.print(String.format(" %2d", 38));
                System.out.println();
                System.out.print(String.format("%-8s", "Bill"));
                System.out.print(String.format(" %2d", 6));
                System.out.println();
                System.out.print(String.format("%-8s", "Trish"));
                System.out.print(String.format(" %2d", 55));
                System.out.println();
                System.out.print(String.format("%-8s", "Jill"));
                System.out.print(String.format(" %2d", 21));
                System.out.println();
        }
}
```

When this program is run it will output:

```
Eric     38
Bill      6
Trish    55
Jill     21
```

As you can see there is considerable repetition in the above code. Also, say you wish to add a ":" to separate the name and the age you would need to modify 4 lines of code. In such a case the use of a method will help greatly. The common part of this code is grouped into a method (called "printNameAndAge"). And the program becomes:

```java
public class ShortNamesList {

        private static void printNameAndAge(String name, int age) {
                System.out.print(String.format("%-8s", name));
                System.out.print(String.format(" %2d", age));
                System.out.println();
        }

        public static void main(String[] args) {
                printNameAndAge("Eric",38);
                printNameAndAge("Bill",6);
                printNameAndAge("Trish",55);
                printNameAndAge("Jill",21);
```

16

```
            }
    }
```

This new program outputs exactly the same lines, however, it is now a little shorter. Also if you wished to add a ":" to separate the name and the age you would need to modify 1 line of code. This modification would effect all of the lines printed.

When a program starts running it begins executing code in the 'main' method. So in the above example, the first line of code executed is "printNameAndAge("Eric",38);". To execute this line of code the program leaves the main method and starts executing the code in the "printNameAndAge" method. When this call is made the parameters of the "printNameAndAge" method are set (name to "Eric" and age to 38). The "printNameAndAge" method is executed line by line and "Eric 38" is printed. Once this method has finished the executing method 'returns' to the main method and continues where it left off. The second line in the main method calls "printNameAndAge" again but this time with 'name' set to "Bill" and age set to 6.

3.2. Methods returning a value

You may also create methods that return a value. The type of data returned by a method is given just before the methods name. So in the example below the 'getRadius' method returns a double, in this case the double is the radius the user typed into the dialog that the method pops up. Whereas, the 'reportAreaCircle' method in the example below returns a String which is a report on the area of the radius provided. Within a method the 'return' statement is used to stop code executing in the method are return the value. In the example of the previous section the 'printNameAndAge' method does not return any value, hence its return type is give as 'void' (which means this method does not return a value).

```
import javax.swing.JOptionPane;

public class AreaCircle {
        public static double getRadius() {
            String radiusStr;
            radiusStr = JOptionPane.showInputDialog("Please enter the
radius.");
            double radius;
            radius = Double.parseDouble(radiusStr);
                // used to convert a number give as
                // a string into its double value
            return radius;
        }

        public static double areaCircle(double radius) {
                double area;
                area = Math.PI * radius * radius;
                return area;
        }

        public static String reportAreaCircle(double radius) {
                return "A circle with radius " +
                        String.format("%.2f", radius) +
                        " has area " +
                        String.format("%.2f",areaCircle(radius));
```

17

```
        }
            public static void main(String[] args) {
                double radius;
                radius = getRadius();
                System.out.println(reportAreaCircle(radius));
            }
    }
```

In the example directly above I have broken down the calculation of 'getRadius' into a number statements, however, this can be simplified by combining the required computation into a single expression. e.g.

```
public static double getRadius() {
    return Double.parseDouble(JOptionPane.showInputDialog("Please enter
the radius."));
}
```

Note - In the examples up until this point we have used the 'System.out.println' method for outputting strings to the console. The example above uses the method 'JOptionPane.showInputDialog' to input from the user a string via a dialog box. This combination can be useful for creating simple interactive programs. The 'JOptionPane.showInputDialog' method requires the import statement 'import javax.swing.JOptionPane;'.

3.3. 'if' statement

The 'if' statement enables your program to execute different code in different situations. Below is a template showing the 'if' statement:

```
if (<boolean expression>) {
    <code A>
} else {
    <code B>
}
```

When the 'if' statement is executed the boolean expression within the brackets is first evaluated. If the boolean expression evaluates to true then <code A> is executed, otherwise if the boolean evaluates to false <code B> is executed.

Example: Suppose your program has a variable that measures the amount of fuel left in a car, denoted 'fuel'. If the amount of fuel runs below 5.0 litres then you wish to alert the user that you are running out of fuel, otherwise, you wish to just say the amount of fuel. This could be done with:

```
if (fuel < 5.0) {
    System.out.println("Fuel running low!!");
} else {
    System.out.println("Fuel currently : " + fuel);
}
```

The 'if' statement can also be used without the else part. In such a situation the code is executed if the boolean evaluates to true and the code is skipped if the boolean evaluates to false. So the above example could be modified such that the alert only

18

happens when the fuel is low:

```
if (fuel < 5.0) {
    System.out.println("Fuel running low!!");
}
```

In some cases you may have many alternatives. A number of 'if-else' statements can be used to deal with multiple alternatives. There are a few ways of organising the 'if-else' statements (see additional material at the end of this chapter), however, it is good to get in the habit of always doing it the same way. The most common way of organising a number of 'if-else' statements is to place a new 'if-else' directly after the last else. An example of this is given below. Using such a template means that only one of the alternate blocks of code is executed, this block will be the first block that has it's boolean evaluate to true. The last block acts as a default (when all the boolean expression evaluate to false).

```
if (fuel <= 0.0) {
    System.out.println("Fuel empty!!!!!");
} else if (fuel < 5.0) {
    System.out.println("Fuel running low!!");
} else if (fuel < 35.0) {
    System.out.println("Fuel currently : " + fuel);
} else {
    System.out.println("Fuel full");
}
```

3.4. 'while' statement

The 'while' statement enables you to repeat (or loop around) the same block of code a number of times. So in the template below <code> will be executed while the boolean expression evaluates to true. Note that each time around the loop the boolean expression is re-evaluated before the block of code is executed.

```
while (<boolean expression>) {
    <code>
}
```

Example : The below code prints the numbers 0 to 9.

```
int i=0;
while (i < 10) {
    System.out.println(i);
    i++;
}
```

Example : This code sums the numbers given via a message dialog.

```
int sum = 0;
String numStr
numStr = JOptionPane.showInputDialog("Next number to sum (or type 'sum'
to sum the numbers and quit) : ");
while (!numStr.equals("sum")) {
    sum = sum + Integer.parseInt(numStr);
    numStr = JOptionPane.showInputDialog("Next number to sum (or type
'sum' to sum the numbers and quit) : ");
}
System.out.println("The total sum is : " + sum);
```

19

While loops will go around 0 or more times. They are often used when before entering the looping code the program does not know the number of times the loop will go around. Note if the boolean expression always evaluates to true then the loop will never end!

3.5. 'for' statement

The 'for' statement is a looping statement like the 'while' loop, however, it is a more structured loop and is often used if you know the number of times the loop will iterate and you require an index of some form. This is a very common situation. The template for the 'for' statement is:

```
for(<initialization statement>; <boolean expression>;  <move index onto
the next value>) {
    <code>
}
```

The initialization statement is executed once before the loop commences, the boolean expression is check to be true before the block of code executed (in the same way as the 'while' statement), the "move index onto the next value" is executed after the block of code is run. It is possible to translate the code of any 'for' statement into a 'while' statement. So the template above would translate to:

```
<initialization statement>
while( <boolean expression> ) {
    <code>
    <move index onto the next value>
}
```

The great thing about the 'for' statement is that it puts all this related information on a single line.

Example: Printing out the numbers from 0 to 9.

```
for (int i = 0; i < 10; i++) {
    System.out.println(i);
}
```

Example: Print a list of people's names from an array.

```
for (int i = 0; i < names.length; i++) {
    System.out.println(name[i]);
}
```

3.6. Additional Material

• **Organizing if-else statements**

There are a few ways of organising 'if-else' statements. The standard way would be to add the next 'if' directly after the 'else'. This creates a decision list.

```
if (fuel <= 0.0) {
    System.out.println("Fuel empty!!!!!");
} else if (fuel < 5.0) {
    System.out.println("Fuel running low!!");
} else if (fuel < 35.0) {
    System.out.println("Fuel currently : " + fuel);
} else {
    System.out.println("Fuel full");
}
```

We could also add other 'if-else' statements after the 'if'. So the above code would become:

```
if (fuel < 35.0) {
    if (fuel < 5.0) {
        if (fuel <= 0.0) {
            System.out.println("Fuel empty!!!!!");
        } else {
            System.out.println("Fuel running low!!");
        }
    } else {
        System.out.println("Fuel currently : " + fuel);
    }
} else {
    System.out.println("Fuel full");
}
```

We could form more of a decision tree by having 'if-else' statements after both the 'if' and the 'else'. So in the example we would have:

```
if (fuel < 5.0) {
    if (fuel <= 0.0) {
        System.out.println("Fuel empty!!!!!");
    } else {
        System.out.println("Fuel running low!!");
    }
} else {
    if (fuel <= 35.0) {
        System.out.println("Fuel currently : " + fuel);
    } else {
        System.out.println("Fuel full");
    }
}
```

Also we could use completely separate 'if' statements to achieve the same function:

```
if (fuel <= 0.0) {
    System.out.println("Fuel empty!!!!!");
}
if (fuel < 5.0 && !(fuel <= 0.0)) {
    System.out.println("Fuel running low!!");
```

```
}
if (fuel < 35.0  && !(fuel <= 0.0)  && !(fuel <= 5.0)) {
    System.out.println("Fuel currently : " + fuel);
}
if ( !(fuel <= 0.0)  && !(fuel <= 5.0) && !(fuel < 35.0)) {
    System.out.println("Fuel full");
}
```

All these approaches will print out the same text for a particular amount of fuel. However, when given the option a programmer should always use the first of these. As by doing things the same way each time reduces the chance of error. Also many programmers use the style given in the first example, so by using this style your code is more readable.

4. Lists and Tables

One of the great strengths of Java is the extent and quality of it's libraries. Almost any standard data structure or operation you wish to perform will have a class written for it. One of the focuses of this book is abstract data types and their implementation. Hence we begin by looking at some of the Libraries Java has to offer and how they would be used. This chapter introduces two very useful data types: the list and the table. Both of these have implementations in the standard Java libraries.

Often as a programmer you wish to store an ordered list of items that can vary in length (note an array has a fixed length). The ArrayList provides such a data type. Also a table that can be indexed via a key can be very useful. A the HashMap class enables you to store a table that can be index via a hashable key. We now look at the use of these two classes in detail.

4.1. ArrayList

The ArrayList class implements the List interface (that is it does the things you would expect a list to do). The ArrayList class enables you to store a list of objects. This list can grow and shrink as you add and remove elements.

The first element in the ArrayList has index 0 and the last element in the ArrayList has index (size() - 1).

To use an ArrayList you need to import the library:

```
import java.util.ArrayList;
```

To create an instance of an ArrayList simply:

```
ArrayList list = new ArrayList();
```

You can also state the type of information stored in the list. e.g. say we had a list of String then we may write:

```
ArrayList<String> list = new ArrayList<String>();
```

The main methods an ArrayList<E> has are:

- **int size()** - this is tells you the number of elements in the list.
- **add(E item)** – adds the 'item' to the end of the list.
- **add(int index, E item)** – inserts the 'item' at position 'index' shifting the elements after this position on by one.
- **set(int index, E item)** – replaces the element at 'index' with 'item'.
- **E get(int index)** – returns the element at position 'index'.
- **remove(int index)** – removes the element at position 'index' shifting the elements after this back.
- **remove(E item)** – removes the first instance of 'item' in the list.

23

You often wish to traverse an ArrayList. This can be done in many ways including: using the 'foreach' statement, using a 'for' loop and index, or using a 'while' loop and iterator. Example code for these three approaches is given below. Note the examples assume we have a list of strings called 'list'.

Using the 'foreach' statement - This is the simplest approach for processing each element in a list.

```
for (String str : list) {
    // process the element 'str'.
}
```

Using a standard 'for' loop and index - This is a little more involved then the other approaches, however, this approach is useful when you would like to know the index value when processing elements of the list. Also this approach could easily be modified to: traverse the list in reverse order, traverse every second element, traverse only the first 10 elements, etc.

```
for (int i = 0; i < list.size(); i++) {
    String str = list.get(i);
    // process the element 'str'.
}
```

Using an iterator - Although a little more complex then the 'foreach' statement, the iterator approach gives you a reference to the interator in the loop. This is useful if you wish to remove elements from the list as you iterate over them (see additional material). The 'foreach' statement uses an Iterator to traverse over the list, however, with the 'foreach' statement you do not have access to the iterator object.

```
Iterator<String> it = list.iterator();
while(it.hasNext()) {
    String str = it.next();
    // process the element 'str'.
}
```

Generally you should use the simplest method that will be sufficient for your programming needs. So in the case of processing elements of an ArrayList if you just need to traverse each element (without removing or knowing the index of the element on the way) just use the 'foreach' statement.

Below is an example of creating an ArrayList of String and using a number of the features mentioned.

```
/*
 * ArrayListExample - a  basic example of using an ArrayList
 * @author Eric McCreath 2006
 */


import java.util.ArrayList;
import java.util.Iterator;

public class ArrayListExample {

        public static void main(String[] args) {
                ArrayList<String> list = new ArrayList<String>();
                list.add("Hello");
```

24

```
list.add("Bye");
list.add("Cat");
list.add("Dog");
list.add("Mouse");
System.out.println("list : " + list);
list.add(1,"Fred");
System.out.println("list : " + list);
list.set(3,"Bill");
System.out.println("list : " + list);
System.out.println(" second " + list.get(1));
list.remove(2);
System.out.println("list : " + list);
list.remove("Mouse");
System.out.println("list : " + list);

for (String str : list) {
        System.out.println("foreach : " + str);
}

for (int i = 0; i< list.size();i++) {
        String str = list.get(i);
        System.out.println("standard for : " + i + " :
" + str);
}

Iterator<String> it = list.iterator();
while(it.hasNext()) {
        String str = it.next();
        System.out.println("iterator : " + str);
}
        }
}
```

4.2. HashMap

Often you wish to maintain a table of objects that you can lookup quickly via a key. For example you may store student records and index them via the student number. The HashMap class implements an indexed table.

Adding new elements into the table is done in constant time (as the table gets bigger the time this operation takes remains the same). Looking up values in the table with the key may also be done in constant time. This is much better than storing the information in an ArrayList. Looking up 1 value will require looking at on average half the values of the ArrayList before the correct one is found!

Suppose you wish to store a list of student's information. This information you also wish to lookup one by one. This could be done either via an ArrayList or a HashMap. The HashMap approach would be better due to the speed in which you could look up elements. The figure below shows data stored using these two approaches.

25

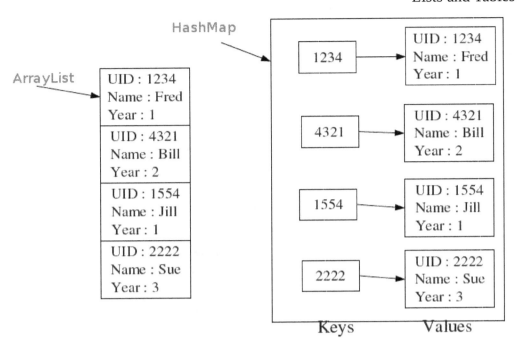

Once again, like the ArrayList class, you need to import this class:

```
import java.util.HashMap;
```

When you declare a variable and create a new instance of HashMap you can state the type of the keys and the type of the values.

```
HashMap<String,Student> hm;
hm = new HashMap<String,Student>();
```

To add new mappings into the hashmap you use the 'put' method.

```
hm.put("u1234", new Student("Fred",1));
hm.put("u4321", new Student("Bill",2));
```

If you put a different value in with the same key then it will go over the top of the current value with that key. Hence when you use a HashMap your index (or key) should be unique.

To use the index to get them our you can use the 'get' method. The below example would assign the student 'Bill' to stu1.

```
stu1 = hm.get("u4321");
```

For HashMap to work the type of the key class must:

- have the 'equals' method implemented, and
- the 'hashCode()' implemented.

Integer, Double, and String have these methods implemented, and hence they are simple types to use for the key. However, if you used your own new class as the key you may need to implement the equals and hashCode methods for your new class.

The 'keySet' method can be used to traverse all the keys in a hash map. The following would print out each entry in the has map. Note, there is no guarantee on the order these entries would be returned in.

```java
for (String key : hm.keySet()) {
    Student value = hm.get(key);
    System.out.println(key + " => " + value);
}
```

The below example stores a postcodes for different locations.

```java
import java.util.HashMap;

/**
 *
 * HashMapExample - This provides an example of using the
 * HashMap class.  In this example we are
 * storing post codes based on the suburb name.
 * @author Eric McCreath
 *
 */

public class HashMapExample {
    public static void main(String[] args) {

        HashMap<String,String> hm = new HashMap<String,String>();

        hm.put("Kaleen","7162");
        hm.put("Chifley","2608");
        hm.put("Acton","2601");

        System.out.println(hm.get("Chifley"));
        System.out.println(hm.get("Kaleen") );

        hm.put("Kaleen","2617");   // lets fix Kaleen!!

        System.out.println(hm.get("Kaleen") );

        for (String key : hm.keySet()) {
            String value = hm.get(key);
            System.out.println(key + " => " + value);
        }
        System.out.println(hm.get("1"));
            // What happens if there is no entry?
    }
}
```

When this code is executed it will print:

```
2608
7162
2617
Acton => 2601
Chifley => 2608
Kaleen => 2617
null
```

27

4.3. Additional Material

Example - Removing Elements Using An Iterator

```
/*
 * IteratorRemoveElementExample
 * @author Eric McCreath 2009
 */


import java.util.ArrayList;
import java.util.Iterator;

public class IteratorRemoveElementExample {

        public static void main(String[] args) {

                // make a list and add some numbers to it
                ArrayList<Integer> list = new ArrayList<Integer>();
                list.add(2);
                list.add(5);
                list.add(7);
                list.add(4);
                list.add(1);
                list.add(22);
                list.add(23);

                System.out.println("before list : " + list);

                // remove the even elements from the list
                Iterator<Integer> it = list.iterator();
                while(it.hasNext()) {
                        Integer val = it.next();
                        if (val % 2 == 0) it.remove();
                }

                System.out.println("after list : " + list);
        }
}
```

Example - Using the Scanner Class for Input

In this example we input a sequence of integers and print 2 times their value as we go.
Any text string indicates the end of inputing.

```
import java.util.Scanner;

public class ScannerExample {

        /**
         * ScannerExample - a simple example of inputting integers
         *                  using a Scanner
         * Eric McCreath 2009
         */
        public static void main(String[] args) {
                Scanner scan = new Scanner(System.in);
```

28

```
System.out.println("Please type in some integers " +
        "and then any text once you have done:");
while (scan.hasNextInt()) {
        int val = scan.nextInt();
        System.out.println((val * 2));
}
    }
}
```

5. Objects and Classes

Java is an object oriented programming language. The idea of an object oriented programming language is to bind together both data and methods into single objects. This enables the programmer to create new data types in which the implementation details of these data types can be hidden from the programmer that is using these new data types. These data types are called 'classes' and instances of them are called 'objects'.

A class is a template (or plan) for an object in Java. Effectively classes represent a 'type'. These 'types' bring together both the state information (fields) and the way the information is manipulated (methods). This is very useful for a number of reasons:

- It enables you to hide the details of the implementation from the user of the class.
- The class implementer defines exactly how the information in the class can be used.
- It also helps produce robust code as a programmer can focus on a particular class.
- Code reuse is often possible.

A class is like a rubber stamp that provides space for information to be filled in. Objects are like a section of paper that has been stamped - once you have done the stamping you can fill in the details. Suppose we have a rubber stamp that is used for labeling an exam paper as 'passed'. The rubber stamp has the following : 'PASS' in big letters; 'name:' and some space to write the examiners name; 'sign:' and a place to sign it; and 'date:' and a place to write the date. Although there would be only one stamp, it would get used many times, also different information would be written on the available space in different cases. This is depicted in the below figure. In the same way a class you design has fields (like the space to write something in the stamp example). Also you normally make many objects from the one class. The fields within these objects would generally be filled in with different information.

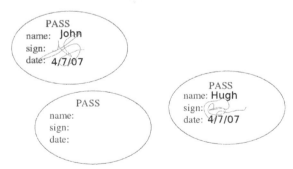

Lets consider a simple example of storing information about a student and their marks. Suppose you wish to be able to store a student's: first name, last name, student number, and final mark. Also you wish to be able to both calculate the final grade and generate a short report on the student. So what you can do is create a new class, called 'Student', which combines the 'data' and 'methods' for a student. The code for this new class is placed in a separated file called 'Student.java':

```java
public class Student {
    /*
     * Student - this class stores and processes
     *               information about a single student
     * Eric McCreath 2009
     */

    // fields
    String firstName;
    String lastName;
    String studentNumber;
    int finalMark;

    // constructor method
    public Student(String fn, String ln, String sn, int fm) {
        this.firstName = fn;
        this.lastName = ln;
        this.studentNumber = sn;
        this.finalMark = fm;
    }

    // methods
    public String grade() {
        if (finalMark < 50) {
            return "N";
        } else if (finalMark < 60) {
            return "P";
        } else if (finalMark < 70) {
            return "C";
        } else if (finalMark < 80) {
            return "D";
        } else {
            return "HD";
        }
    }
    public String report() {
        return "Name : " + lastName + "n" +
               "UID : " + studentNumber + "n" +
               "Final Mark : " + finalMark + "n" +
               "Grade : " + grade() + "n";
    }
}
```

Lets look at each part of this Student class. The very first line has:

- **public** - which means this new data type is intended to be used by external code (or other classes).
- **class** - this is a new class or data type that we are defining.
- **Student** - is name of this new class. Note generally class names should be nouns and start with an upper case letter.

All the code for the class is then enclosed in curly brackets.

The next part of this class is a comment which provides a short summary of the class along with authorship details. Note this is important as it gives someone reading the class a quick summary of what the class is about and the details of who wrote it.

The next section of code is the fields of the class. This is the data that is stored in each instance (or object) of the class. The methods of the class that are executed on a particular object of the class can directly access these fields. They are defined in the same way you would define a local variable within a method.

The "constructor method" is a special method that is executed when creating a new instance of the class. In this example we simply initialise the fields of this particular object. Note the constructor method has the same name as the class and has no return type. It is possible to give a number of different constructor methods, also if no constructor method is given then Java provides a default one which initialises all of the fields to 'null' or '0'.

The final section of code contains two methods 'grade' and 'report'. These methods are always executed in the context of a particular object.

Now that we have our new class we need to use it. To use it we need to construct objects which are instances of the class. This is done via the 'new' keyword. This is know as instanciating the class or constructing objects of the class. A constructor method is executed when constructing a new object (either one specified via the class or a default one is used if none are specified). We can define variables that reference these objects. So in the example below we have the variable stu1 which references an object of type Student.

```
| Student stu1;
```

We can construct a new object of type Student.

```
| stu1 = new Student("Hugh", "Bonsor", "u1234567", 81);
```

In this case the constructor method will initialise the fields in the object. We can construct a number of these objects based on a single class. Although they will all have the same 'structure' they will generally hold different information. To continue the above example we construct another student named Eric who has not gained such a high mark.

```
| Student stu2 = new Student("Eric", "McCreath", "u7654321", 62);
```

In the machines memory the Java virtual machine has created two objects. One has info about 'Hugh' the other 'Eric'. The variables 'stu1' and 'stu2' provide a reference to these objects. You can image these references to be like pointers. Note you can have two different references pointing to the same object. Also when an object has nothing referencing it then it is effectively unavailable to the program and the Java Virtual Machine (JVM) will use its garbage collector to reclaim the memory.

We could add an other variable, 'stu3', which also references the object which stores Eric's information.

```
| Student stu3 = stu2;
```

This could be depicted as :

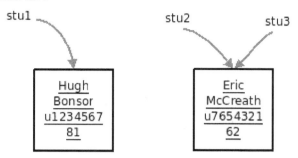

The '.' operator may be used to execute a method for a particular object. So in our example if we executed the code:

```
System.out.println(stu1.grade());
```

it would execute the 'grade' method on the object that has Hugh's information. The grade method for Hugh would return the string 'HD' and hence the above code would printout "HD". However, if we executed the code:

```
System.out.println(stu2.grade());
```

It would execute the same piece of code, but, on a different object. Namely on the object that contains Eric's information. If you look at the code for 'grade' it reads the 'field' finalMark to determine what grade to return. The value of finalMark will depend on the object grade is executed in reference to. So methods get executed in the context of the data of a particular object.

Also the '.' operator may be used to obtain a reference to the fields of a particular object. So if you executed the code:

```
System.out.println(stu3.lastName);
```

it would print 'McCreath'. Also the '.' operator can be used for modifying fields of a particular object. So if you executed the code:

```
stu2.finalMark = 61;
```

it would set Eric's finalMark to 61.

Understanding the concept to classes and objects is central for programming in Java. These ideas are built on and extended as we look at inheritance and interfaces, so it is important students go over this section and take time to digest the these ideas.

5.1. UML Class Diagrams

UML (Unified Modeling Language) is a standard way of describing a program's design. In this text we are focusing on UML Class Diagrams, however, there is a lot more to UML that we will not look at. UML Class Diagrams provide a simple way of describing: the classes that make up your program, the fields and methods of the classes, and the way classes relate to each other. These diagrams will not contain any code, this is left for the program.

A Class is pictorially described using a rectangle along with the Class name in the middle of it. So below is an UML Class Diagram that shows the student class:

```
+--------------------------------+
|                                |
|           Student              |
|                                |
+--------------------------------+
```

This is a very coarse level of design. However, it is helpful to first think of the classes you need and their names and how they relate. Once this is done the designer can refine the UML class diagram and add more detail (like fields and methods). To add fields and methods the rectangle is partitioned into three sections: the first gives the class name, the second the fields, and the third the methods. So our Student class would look like:

```
+--------------------------------+
|            Student             |
+--------------------------------+
| +firstName: String             |
| +lastName: String              |
| +studentNumber: String         |
| +finalMark: int                |
+--------------------------------+
| +grade(): String               |
| +report(): String              |
+--------------------------------+
```

Note that the syntax is a little different then that of Java. So for fields we have "<field name> : <field type>", and for methods we have "<method name>(<parameters>) : <return type>". We also can describe the relationship between classes. The main relationship we will use in this text are:

- **aggregation** (a class is made up of another class) This is a 'has a' relationship. That is when a line connects two class with an empty diamond then objects of one class are made up of objects of the other class. So in the example below a TutorialGroup 'has a' or is made up of objects of type Student. Note we see the type Student in the fields of TutorialGroup, this is expected for aggregation. The location of the diamond is next to the class that is made up of the connecting class. Aggregation is a type of association.

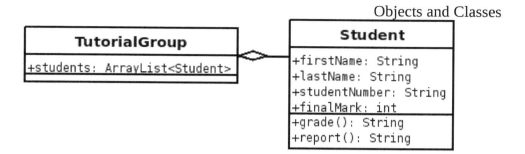

- **dependency** (a class uses another class) This is a 'uses' relationship. This is depicted with a dashed line and a simple arrow head. Suppose we have a class that logs text entries to a log file, called Logger, the current date is added to all these log entries. This Logger class may use the Date class for adding to the log entries, but it would not store any Date objects. So it is not aggregation, but, there is a dependency (i.e. our logger would not work without help from the date class). Notice how there is no 'Date' type mentioned in the Logger fields.

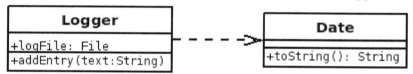

- **generalization** (a class inherits from the other class) This is a 'is a' relationship. And is depicted with an unfilled arrow head. Note we have not looked at generalization and realises yet, they will be explained in a later chapter.

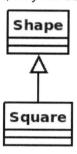

- **realises** (a class implements the interface for another class) This is a 'does a' relationship. And is depicted with an unfilled arrow head and a dashed line.

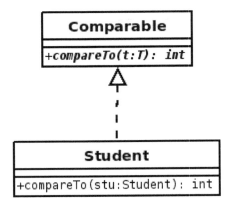

There are a number of tools for drawing these diagrams, these will also often have ways of automatically generating code that can then have the implementation details added. Note that UML is not especially for Java, and although it embraces most of the design aspects in Java, it is not always a perfect match. However, this is okay as it is only a tool for sketching out a design.

The tool that I have used with the above UML Class Diagrams is called 'dia', see http://www.gnome.org/projects/dia/. Under Files->Plugins there is a box you can tick for UML which gives you options for drawing UML. Also 'umbrello' is a useful tool for drawing UML diagrams (although I have found dia simpler and is less prone to crashing as I have found umbrello to do).

The Wikipedia has a helpful overview of class diagrams.
http://en.wikipedia.org/wiki/Class_diagram

5.2. Static fields and methods

Every time an instance of a class is created, that is an object, memory is allocated for the fields in the object. However, sometimes you wish to have data common to all the objects of the class. This is done using the 'static' keyword.

In our 'rubber stamp' analogy a static field is like a label on the back of the rubber stamp that you may write information on. You only have one copy of this data for each rubber stamp, rather then one copy per piece of paper you stamp onto. In the same way you only have one copy of a static field for each class you have, rather than one per object which is the case for non-static fields.

In a similar way static methods are not executed in the context of a particular object. Rather they execute in the context of the parameters they are given and the static fields of the class.

To read or set a static field you use: the class name, a dot '.', and then the static field name. Given the following code:

```
public class A {
    static int y;
    int x;
}
```

Then if we executed:

```
A o1, o2, o3;
o1 = new A();
o2 = new A();
o3 = new A();
o2.x = 11;
A.y = 7;
```

We could depict the information stored by Java as:

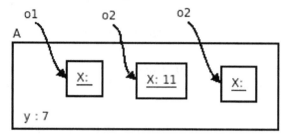

6. Inheritance, Interfaces, and Abstract Classes

Classes provide a way of creating new types of information. This gives the programmer a way of binding together both information (the fields) and process (the methods) into a single coherent entity, called a class. Sometimes you may wish to implement a class that is very similar to a class that is already implemented. Clearly this could be done simply by duplicating the class (i.e. cut and paste) and making the required modifications. This approach has a number of drawbacks including:

- as the code is duplicated we end up with more code to maintain,
- if any errors are in the original code we end up with a copy of those errors thus creating more work for debugging and testing of the code, and
- modifications/additions of the overlapping code need to be mirrored in the original code.

Another approach is to leave the original class and create a new class that refers to the original class and only include code that extends/changes the original code. This is called inheritance.

It is important to get a good understanding of the idea of inheritance as it provides a very useful way of making use of existing code. It also provides a good starting point for understanding interfaces and abstract classes.

6.1. Inheritance

So for example say we had a class called Person which stored information about a person along with a method for printing their details. The Java code would be:

```
public class Person {
        String firstName;
        String lastName;
        public Person(String fn, String ln) {
                firstName = fn;
                lastName = ln;
        }
        public Person() {
        }
        public String show() {
                return firstName + " " + lastName;
        }
        public String initials() {
                return firstName.substring(0, 1).toUpperCase() +
                        lastName.substring(0, 1).toUpperCase();
        }
}
```

Now if we wish to create a new class called Student. Student is very similar to a Person having: firstName, lastName, and show(), however, we also wish to have studentNumber. In Java we can create the Student class by extending the Person class. To do this we use the 'extends' keyword and we would say Student inherits from Person. The Student code would be:

```
public class Student extends Person {
        String uniId;
        public Student(String fn, String ln, String ui) {
                firstName = fn;
                lastName = ln;
                uniId = ui;
        }
        public boolean checkUid() {
                // a simple check that it is a valid uni id
                return uniId.length() == 8 && uniId.charAt(0) == 'u';
        }
}
```

This new Student class has all of the methods and fields of the Person class plus the 'uniId' field and the 'checkUid' method. So for example if we create a new Student object we can make use of all method/fields of Person.

```
Student stu = new Student("Hugh","McCreath","u1234567");
System.out.println(stu.initials());   // would print HM
```

We would say a Student 'is a' Person. These classes can also be shown using a UML Class diagram.

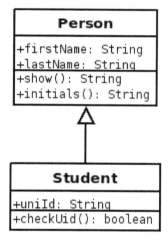

If class B extends (inherits from) class A then, in terms of their type, class B is a specialisation of class A. However, in terms of their behaviour/function/information class B adds to class A. The new class will have all the original methods and fields of the class it extends. You can add to these fields and methods.

When you construct a child class you often wish to use the parents constructor. This can be done with the 'super' key word. This must be done at the beginning of the constructor. The below example modifies the Student class to make use of the constructor method in Person.

```
public class Student extends Person {
        String uniId;
        public Student(String fn, String ln, String ui) {
                super(fn,ln);
```

```
            uniId = ui;
        }
        public boolean checkUid() { // a simple check that it is a
valid uni id
            return uniId.length() == 8 && uniId.charAt(0) == 'u';
        }
    }
```

If you wish to modify a method of the parent class then you can simply **override** it. This simply involves writing a method in the child class with the same signature as the parent. When the method is call on an object, of the child, the child's method is used. In the example below we modify the Student class and override the 'show' method of Person.

```
public class Student extends Person {
    String uniId;
    public Student(String fn, String ln, String ui) {
        super(fn,ln);
        uniId = ui;
    }
    public boolean checkUid() {
            // a simple check that it is a valid uni id
        return uniId.length() == 8 && uniId.charAt(0) == 'u';
    }
    public String show() {
        return firstName + " " + lastName + " : " + uniId;
    }
}
```

In the above example when the show method is executed on a Student then the show method in Student is used.

```
Student stu = new Student("Hugh","McCreath","u1234567");
System.out.println(stu.show()); // prints "Hugh McCreath : u1234567"
```

In some cases when you override a method it is useful to also be able to execute the parent's method. In this way you can do what is normally done along with some modification. So to produce the same result for the 'show' method in Student we could have done:

```
public String show() {
    return super.show() + " : " + uniId;
}
```

6.2. Abstract Classes

Sometimes a class is designed to be a template for other classes. It is not designed to have any real instances (objects) created from it. These are called abstract classes.

Abstract classes are designed to be extended. The classes that extend an abstract class will usually be standard classes that can construct real objects.

Abstract classes can have abstract methods that only have the signature and not the implementation.

A common approach to design is to have a abstract class with a number of different children. These children are types of the parent abstract class.

Suppose we are implementing a drawing program that can draw different shapes on a screen. The shapes could include a Square, a Circle, and a Triangle. These all have things that are common, like say the color or the location on the screen they are drawn, however, they also have a number of aspects that are different (a circle has a radius whereas a square has a side length) also they are all drawn differently. One design approach is to create an abstract class that has what is in common and then the Square, Triangle and Circle classes are individual classes that extend this one abstract class Shape.

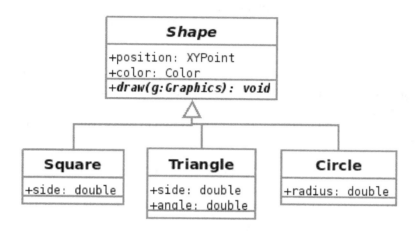

Lets now have a look at the code for the abstract class Shape:

```
import java.awt.Color;
import java.awt.Graphics;

public abstract class Shape {
        XYPoint position;
        Color color;

        public abstract void draw(Graphics g);
}
```

Notice how the 'abstract' key word is used in both defining the class and the single method that is abstract in the class. This keyword, abstract, carries with it the idea of a 'template'. So the class can not directly create objects of type Shape, also the abstract method gives the signature but no code. The code will (and must) come in a class that extends this abstract class. In this case we have the class Square extending from Shape:

```
import java.awt.Color;
import java.awt.Graphics;

public class Square extends Shape {
        double side;

        public Square(Color c, XYPoint p, double s) {
                side = s;
```

```
                color = c;
                position = p;
        }

        public void draw(Graphics g) {
                g.setColor(color);
                g.drawRect((int) position.getX(),
                        (int) position.getY(),
                        (int) side, (int) side);
        }
}
```

Notice how the signature for the method draw is the same as that of draw defined in Shape. Also this method has access to the fields position and color from Shape.

6.3. Interfaces

Java only allows single inheritance. However, in some situation you would like a class to take on the characteristics of multiple classes. So for example our Student, defined above, we may wish to be able to order, or rank, them in some way. By the use of an interface we can say a Student is able to be compared in a standard way, thus we can make use of standard methods such as sorting to help organise our students. This saves us re-implement a sorting routine just for the student class. Lets see what the code will look like.

```
public class Student extends Person implements Comparable<Student> {
        String uniId;
        public Student2(String fn, String ln, String ui) {
                firstName = fn;
                lastName = ln;
                uniId = ui;
        }
        public boolean checkUid() {
                        // a simple check that it is a valid uni id
                return uniId.length() == 8 && uniId.charAt(0) == 'u';
        }

        public String show() {
                return super.show() + " : " + uniId;
        }

        public int compareTo(Student other) {
                return uniId.compareTo(other.uniId);
        }
}
```

The name of the interface for doing ordering is called "Comparable" and requires a method implemented called "compareTo" which returns a positive integer if the "other" student ranks before this student, 0 if they rank the same, and negative if the other student ranks after this one. In the above example we just compare the student id for comparing different students, however, we could also rank on last name, or mark if we stored this information. We would say that a Student 'is a' Person, but also we can say Student 'does a' Comparable. In terms of the type of a Student it is both a Person and a Comparable. So the sort method in the Collections class can sort an ArrayList of Comparable things, hence, if we have an ArrayList of Student, it can also be viewed as

42

an ArrayList of Comparable and hence we can use the standard sort methods. This is shown in the example below which when executed would re-order the ArrayList (to Matthew, Hugh, and John):

```
ArrayList<Student> list = new ArrayList<Student>();
list.add(new Student("Hugh","McCreath","u1234567"));
list.add(new Student("John","McCreath","u7654321"));
list.add(new Student("Matthew","McCreath","u1111111"));
Collections.sort(list);
```

So Interfaces provide a way of very different classes implementing the same methods. The interface defines the signatures of the methods used. These methods are implicitly all abstract. That is no implementation is given. The implementation must be done in the class that implements the interface. Interfaces may also contain constants. These constants are implicitly public, static, and final.

The code for the standard Comparable interface is:

```
public abstract interface Comparable {
    public abstract int compareTo(Object arg0);
}
```

At times it is useful to be able to create your own interfaces. They are best used when different types of classes share some common characteristic. So for example you may define a interface called Drawable (has a method draw) which is implement by a number of very different classes. Objects of all these classes could be added to a drawing list which could be drawn as required.

A class can implement a number of interfaces. The interfaces a class implements are simply listed after the 'implements' keyword using a comma separated list.

7. Useful Java Classes

7.1. Random

Objects of this class generate a sequence of pseudo-random numbers. This can be used in a class to initialize a random initial state. It can also be used to make a class act randomly.

To obtain random numbers you first need to import the Random class:

```
import java.util.Random;
```

The following creates a new instance of the random class.

```
static Random rand = new Random();
```

This can be done within a class as a static variable, this means you only have one Random object from which all the objects in the class obtain their random numbers. Alternatively you could have one Random object for each object that requires random numbers (generating lots of objects of this Random class). Also you could have one Random object for the entire project (this would increase coupling and would make code less reusable).

Obtaining a random double, uniformly distributed between 0.0 and 1.0, can be achieved by :

```
double r = rand.nextDouble();
```

To obtain a random integer which can take on the values 0,1,2, … n-1 you can simply do:

```
int i = rand.nextInt(n);
```

7.2. Date and SimpleDateFormat

The Date class provides objects that store the time and date with millisecond precision. To import the Date class simply:

```
import java.util.Date;
```

The following will construct a new Date object that is set to the current time:

```
Date d = new Date();
```

Date also has a toString() method which enables you to display the date. Note that, the format of this method is fix. You can also compare dates with the 'before', 'after', 'equals', and 'compareTo' methods.

The SimpleDateFormat class enables easy formatting and parsing of dates. This is useful as dates can be formatted in many different ways. This class needs to be imported:

```
import java.text.SimpleDateFormat;
```

Objects of this class are used for formatting and parsing. The constructor of this class may be provided with the date format you desire. The example below has the date first with day, month and year and then time in 24 hours.

```
SimpleDateFormat df = new SimpleDateFormat("d/M/yyyy k:m");
```

Once an object of SimpleDateFormat is created it can be used to format a date (converting it from Date to String). For example the following would return the current date and time as a String formatted according to the df's setup.

```
df.format(new Date())
```

The same SimpleDateFormat object can be used to parse a String into a Date. The following would return a Date object set to 1:30pm 22nd Nov 2002.

```
df.parse("22/11/2002 13:30")
```

If the string given for parsing is incorrectly formatted then a ParseException is thrown.

7.3. JFrame

The JFrame class provides the main window for a Graphical User Interface (GUI). The JFrame is like an empty window that you can: add components, add menus, and set preferences. There are a few different ways of setting up a JFrame. These include:

- having your main GUI program extend a JFrame,

- having the JFrame as a variable within a main method, or

- having a class which embraces the state of your GUI and having a JFrame as a field within in this.

An example of the last of these approaches is now given.

This example is a simple GUI that just says "Hello World!". It provides a simple template to start with when you are writing your own application.

```
import java.lang.String;

import javax.swing.JFrame;
import javax.swing.JLabel;

public class JFrameDemo {

        JFrame jframe;

        public JFrameDemo() {
                jframe = new JFrame("JFrameDemo");
                jframe.setDefaultCloseOperation(JFrame.EXIT_ON_CLOSE);
                (jframe.getContentPane()).add(
                                new JLabel("Hello World"));
                jframe.pack();
                jframe.setVisible(true);
        }
```

```
public static void main(String[] args) {
        JFrameDemo demo;
        demo = new JFrameDemo();
    }
}
```

7.4. JComponent

Objects of the JComponent Class are components that can be added to a JFrame. These components are like blank drawing areas (hence the name).

There is a number of standard class that extend the JComponent class. Including:

- JButton - buttons that you can press,
- JLabel - show some text or an image,
- JTextArea - a box with some editable text,
- JList - a selection list, and
- JPanel - a generally purpose container, often used to layout a number of other component.

If the standard components are not what you are looking for your can create your own. To do this you would normally create your own class that extends the JComponent class and overwrite the 'paint' method along with adding any other features you would like.

The below example builds on the JFrameDemo creating a very simple drawing program.

```
import java.awt.BorderLayout;
import java.awt.Color;
import java.awt.Dimension;
import java.awt.Graphics;
import java.awt.event.ActionEvent;
import java.awt.event.ActionListener;
import java.awt.event.MouseEvent;
import java.awt.event.MouseMotionListener;
import java.awt.image.BufferedImage;

import javax.swing.JButton;
import javax.swing.JColorChooser;
import javax.swing.JComponent;
import javax.swing.JFrame;
import javax.swing.JPanel;

public class SimpleDraw implements ActionListener, MouseMotionListener
{

        JFrame jframe;
        JComponent canvas;
        JButton clearButton;
        JColorChooser colorChooser;
        JPanel mainPanel;
        BufferedImage image;

        static final Dimension dim = new Dimension(500,300);
```

46

```
public SimpleDraw() {
        // make and set up all the components
        image = new BufferedImage(dim.width,dim.height,
                                    BufferedImage.TYPE_INT_RGB);
        canvas = new JComponent() {
                public void paint(Graphics g) {
                        g.drawImage(image, 0, 0, null);
                }
        }; // This is a tricky way of creating a new class that
           // extends the JComponent class without giving it a
           // name or having to create a new java file.
        canvas.setPreferredSize(dim);
        colorChooser = new JColorChooser();
        clearButton = new JButton("clear");
        clearButton.addActionListener( this);
        canvas.addMouseMotionListener( this);

        // make and add components to the panel
        mainPanel = new JPanel(new BorderLayout());
        mainPanel.add(canvas,BorderLayout.CENTER);
        mainPanel.add(colorChooser,BorderLayout.EAST);
        mainPanel.add(clearButton,BorderLayout.NORTH);

        // set up the JFrame
        jframe = new JFrame("SimpleDraw");
        jframe.setDefaultCloseOperation(JFrame.EXIT_ON_CLOSE);
        (jframe.getContentPane()).add(mainPanel);
        jframe.pack();
        jframe.setVisible(true);
}

public static void main(String[] args) {
        SimpleDraw demo;
        demo = new SimpleDraw();
}

public void actionPerformed(ActionEvent event) {
        if (event.getSource() == clearButton) {
                Graphics g = image.getGraphics();
                g.setColor(Color.white);
                g.fillRect(0, 0, dim.width, dim.height);
                canvas.repaint();
        }
}

public void mouseDragged(MouseEvent event) {
        if (event.getSource() == canvas) {
                Graphics g = image.getGraphics();
                g.setColor(colorChooser.getColor());
                g.fillRect(event.getX()-1,
                            event.getY()-1, 3, 3);
                canvas.repaint();
        }
}

public void mouseMoved(MouseEvent event) {
}
}
```

7.5. Graphics

The **Graphics** class provides a set of methods for drawing to a raster (or bitmap) display/object. Objects of the **Graphics** class maintain the current drawing state, this state information includes the current drawing colour and the current font in use. The class includes methods for drawing: lines, ovals boarders, filled ovals, rectangle boarders, filled rectangles, images, and text. The ovals method can also be used to draw circles.

Coordinates for drawing are given as xy integer values with (0,0) being the top left hand coordinate of the screen. The x values go from left to right and the y values go from top to bottom.

If you wish to draw within a Java GUI then normally you would create a **JComponent** that you add to the **JFrame** of the GUI. Then you would overwrite the 'paint' method of the **JComponent**. The 'paint' method has a reference to a **Graphics** object as an attribute. Drawing to this **Graphics** object will ultimately be rendered to the screen.

Note that, the **Graphics** class you can only draw, you can not use this class to 'see' what you have drawn. If you wish to be able to obtain the colour of the pixels drawn then you should draw to a **BufferedImage** and read the pixel values via this class.

8. Complexity

Different programs take different amounts of time to execute. Also different programs will require different amounts of main memory. A satisfactory implementation of any problem not only must be valid, it also needs to execute within time and memory constraints of the system it is run on.

Thus as you design a solution you need to keep in mind how that solution will scale. Will your solution cope under the expected load?

More than anything else the 'order' of a program/method will determine how well it will scale. This chapter will introduce the idea of the 'order' of a program, more formally this is know as complexity analysis.

8.1. Introduction

There is usually many different solutions to the same problem. They will take different amounts of time to run and use different amounts of memory. You could implement the different approaches and compare their performance. This would give a good indication of what is the best approach. However, a good software engineer will be able to estimate the performance of a program directly from it's design and compare different approaches without implementing anything! This will save a lot of time and also help direct your design and implementation.

Often you wish to check that a program will work in the worst case. This is simplest form of analysis. And is known as worst case analysis. If you know your program will run fast enough in the worst case then it will also run okay in average or normal cases.

A simple approximation of how long a program will take to execute is to count the number of primitive statements executed. Each primitive statement will take a different amount of time to execute on different machines. However, as there is a limited number of primitive statements, all these statements will execute in less than some fixed maximum amount of time. Let us denote this fixed maximum amount of time as $tmax$. Now if our program takes TS primitive statements to execute then the time taken to execute the program will be at most:

$$TS * tmax$$

This is useful as now to get an idea of how long our program will take all we need to do is count the number of primitive statements and know the maximum time for the set of possible primitive statements. Let us show this idea with a simple example. Suppose we have the following method that measures the distance between to xy-points.

```
public double distance(XYPoint p) {
    double xdiff = p.x - x;
    double ydiff = p.y - y;
    return Math.sqrt(xdiff*xdiff + ydiff*ydiff);
```

49

```
| }
```

The number of statements executed when this method is run will be (note the subscript is the name of the method) :

$$TS_{distance} = 3$$

This method will not get any slower for different xy-points. If the slowest primitive statement took 1ms then we would know this method would always execute in less time than 3ms.

The next example is a little more complex. This method calculates the mean of an ArrayList of Doubles.

```java
public class MyList extends ArrayList<Double> {
  public Double mean() {
    Double sum = 0.0;
    for (Double d : this) {
      sum += d;
    }
    return sum/size();
  }
}
```

The number of statements executed will depend of the size of the list. Let n equal the size of the list. So now how long the method takes to execute will be a function of n. The *"for (Double d : this)"* would involve n primitive statements as each time around the loop *'d'* must be assignment to the next element of the list. Also *"sum +=d;"* will get executed n times as it is in the loop. Whereas both *"Double sum = 0.0;"* and *"return sum/size();"* only get executed once each time the method is called. This gives us a total number of steps:

$$TS_{mean}(n) = 2n + 2$$

So if n was *100* and the slowest primitive statement took 1ms then the `mean' method would take at most 202ms. As n gets bigger the *"+2"* part of this calculation becomes insignificant in terms of how long this method takes to run. e.g. if *n=100* then about 99% of the time is spent executing the loop. The idea of the Big-O notation is to focus on the most significant component of the time required to execute the method/program.

You would say the method that calculates the `mean' is of order n (or linear). In big-O notation this would be stated as:

$$TS_{mean}(n) \in O(n)$$

Notice how we dropped the *2* from the *2n* giving us *O(n)*, this is because we wish to focus on the shape of the function rather than be able to give an estimate of actual time.

In the other example you would say the distance method is order 1 (or constant). This would be formally stated as:

$$TS_{distance}(n) \in O(1)$$

8.2. Big-O Formal Definition

The Big-O notation can be formally defined as:

Suppose n is the size of the problem the method is being applied to.

Let $TS(n)$ be the number of primitive statements executed in the method (this is in the worst case for a particular n).

Then we would say:

$$TS(n) \in O(f(n))$$

if and only if

there exists a constant $c > 0$, and a constant $n_0 > 0$, such that for all $n > n_0$ we have:

$$TS(n) \leqslant c * f(n)$$

In the below diagram the *TS(n)* function (this is the count of the primitive statements that are executed for a particular n) is always below the line *c*n* after n_0. In this case our *f(n)=n*. As we can select any *c* and n_o this notation enables us to remove constant and less significant components from our description of how the program scales. In this case we say the program is *O(n)*.

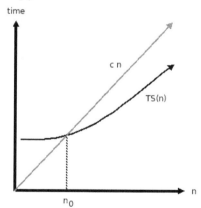

Once again in the below example the line *TS(n)* function is always below the line *c* after n_0. So in this case we say the program is *O(1)*.

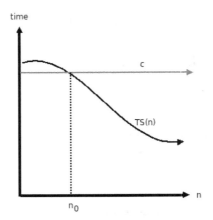

If a method is *O(n)* or *O(1)* then it scales very well and generally any method you implement with such scaling will work okay in almost all situation (exceptions to this may be if latency is very important, or if *n* is very very large - for the *O(n)* case). However, some methods take a lot more time to execute. We now look at such an example.

An Example

Suppose we have an ArrayList of integers and we wish to find the largest gap between any two integers in the list. A simple way of doing this is to compare every integer with every other integer, calculate the gap, and return the maximum over all these gaps. The code for a method which takes a list with *n* elements in it is:

```
static Integer biggestGap(ArrayList<Integer> list) {
  Integer biggestGap = null;   // 1
  for (int i = 0; i < list.size(); i++) { // n
    for (int j = 0; j < list.size(); j++) { // n*n
      int gap = Math.abs(list.get(i) - list.get(j)); // n*n
      if (biggestGap == null || biggestGap < gap) { // n*n
        biggestGap = gap;   // n*n
      }                     // given we are doing worst case
    }                       // analysis we assume the if
  }                         // contition alway evaluates to true
  return biggestGap; // 1
}
```

In the code above the comments show the number of times each statement executes.

So the total number of instructions we would execute would be:

$$TS_{biggestGap}(n) = 4n^2 + n + 2$$

And we would say our 'biggestGap' method is $O(n^2)$ where *n* is the length of the list. Or we would say:

$$TS_{biggestGap}(n) \in O(n^2)$$

We can prove this from the definition. To do this proof we simple find constants c and n_0 such that the inequality holds in the definition.

Lets say $c = 7$ and $n_0 = 1$.

So we are required to show that for all $n > 1$:

$$4n^2 + n + 2 \leqslant 7n^2$$

To show this we work backwards. For we know that for all $n > 1$:

$$1 \leqslant n^2$$
$$2 \leqslant 2n^2$$
$$n + 2 \leqslant n + 2n^2$$
$$n + 2 \leqslant n^2 + 2n^2$$
$$4n^2 + n + 2 \leqslant 4n^2 + n^2 + 2n^2$$
$$4n^2 + n + 2 \leqslant 7n^2 \quad q.e.d.$$

8.3. Aspects to note

- The big-O notation describes a set of functions, this is why the set notation is often used with the big-O notation. More traditionally people used the = symbol rather than the $\in$ symbol, however, this is a misuse of the normal way we would use equals.

- Say we have a program that executes $7n^4 + 3n^2 + 100$ steps, for a particular n. We would normally just say it is $O(n^4)$ as $7n^4 + 3n^2 + 100 \in O(n^4)$. Yet, it is also the case that $7n^4 + 3n^2 + 100 \in O(7n^4)$ or even $7n^4 + 3n^2 + 100 \in O(7n^4 + 3n^2 + 100)$. However, as the idea of the big-O notation is to remove constant and less significant factors you would not include them in your statement on complexity.

- The big-O notation acts as a maximum. So for example it is true that $7n \in O(n^4)$ (one can simply check this from the definition, possible constants are c=7 and n_0=1). However, one would normally give the lowest possible maximum for a particular method or program. So if the number of primitive statements was *7n* then you would normally say such a program is *O(n)*.

- The big-O notation provides a natural way of ranking approaches. A method or program that is O(n) would run faster than one that is $O(n^2)$ (at least for all n larger then some fixed constant). Different complexities can be ordered:

$$O(1) \subset O(\log n) \subset O(n) \subset O(n \log n) \subset O(n^2) \subset$$
$$O(n^{2.376}) \subset O(n^3) \subset O(n^4) \subset O(2^n) \subset O(n!) \subset O(n^n) \subset O(2^{2^n})$$

53

8.4. Tractable and intractable problems.

Some algorithms may take so long to run on a computer for certain problem sizes that it is just not worth implementing them. So for example it may take a modern computer 100 year to find the optimal layout of a particular circuit design, yet, the optimal layout may be of little use in 100 years! Problems for which there is an algorithm, yet, the implementation of the algorithm would take too long to run are said to be intractable. To clarify this division Computer scientists have said that problems for which there is a polynomial solution are considered tractable. And problems for which there is no polynomial solutions are said to be intractable.

So sorting a list can be done in $O(n^2)$ where *n* is the number of elements to sort.[2] So the task of sorting is said to be tractable. Whereas, the task of finding a variable assignments that makes a Boolean formula true (this is known as the Boolean satisfiability problem) does not have a polynomial solution (at least no one has found one yet!). This task of Boolean satisfiability is said to be intractable. Note that Boolean satisfiability is important because it is useful in such tasks as electronic circuit design and formal proofs.

8.5. Complexity with more than one variable

Sometimes you will have algorithms that can change there running time dependant on more than one variable. Now it is possible to include more than one variable within the big-O notation. It is simply a matter of defining the two (or more) variables and then working out the formula that bounds the running time based on these two variables.

Say we are doing matrix multiplication between two matricies, the first is a *n-by-m* matrix and the second is an *m -by-n.* Using the simple algorithm which takes the dot product between rows and columns the complexity would be $O(m^2 n)$. This gives us an idea of the running time of a program that implements the algorithm as the size of the problem changes. If the matricies where square (i.e. n=m) then the complexity would simplify to $O(n^3)$ where n is the number of rows and columns in the matricies. However, if the number of columns of the first matrix was fix (also fixing the number of rows of the second matrix) then the algorithm's complexity would be $O(n)$.

When doing complexity analysis it is important to think about what you wish to measure, and which variable will have the most significant influence on the overall performance.

8.6. Space

Complexity analysis can also be done on the amount of space (or main memory) an

---

2   Sort can be done in $O(n \log n)$ (or even $O(n)$ when some constraints are known about what is being sorted) where *n* is the number of elements being sorted. However, given the big-O notation is like a "maximum" it is still correct to say that sorting can be done in $O(n^2)$.

algorithm will take to complete its execution for a particular sized input. If there is limited main memory and the problem size is very big then space may become the limiting factor. In a similar way to how we evaluation and compare algorithms in terms of their time complexity we can compare them in terms of their space complexity. In some cases there is a trade off in algorithms between time and space.

Lets consider a simple algorithm for determining the maximum number in a list of numbers. This could be implemented with the following:

```
public Integer max(ArrayList<Integer> l) {
        Integer m = null;
        for (Integer i : l) {
                if (m == null || i > m) m = i;
        }
        return m;
}
```

The time complexity of this method is $O(n)$ where n is the number of elements in the list l. If we exclude the storage of the input data, list l, then the amount of memory this method uses does not change as the size of l increases (there is memory for the result value and there would also be some fixed amount of memory used for the foreach loop). Hence the space complexity would be $O(1)$.

Lets now consider the slightly more complex example of find the median element in a list of integers. A simple way of solving such a problem is to first sort the list and then take the middle element of this sorted list. In this case because we do not wish to change the order of the list given to the method we need to clone the list, this will require $O(n)$ space. Also the sort, depending on which algorithm used, will require a certain amount of space, although this would not be more than $O(n)$.

```
public Integer median(ArrayList<Integer> l) {
        ArrayList<Integer> lc = (ArrayList<Integer>) l.clone();
                                        // we need a copy of l
        Collections.sort(lc); // O(n log n) time complexity
        return lc.get(lc.size()/2);
}
```

Overall the time complexity of this method would be $O(n \log n)$ and the space complexity would be $O(n)$. Now if this list was particularly large we may not have enough space for the problem size we are working with. We could attempt to modify the algorithm such that it used less space (but more execution time).

```
static public Integer median(ArrayList<Integer> l) {
        for(Integer i : l) {
                if (isMedian(i,l)) return i;
        }
        return null;
}

static public boolean isMedian(int i, ArrayList<Integer> l) {
        int less = 0;
        int more = 0;
        for(Integer j : l) {
                if (j < i) less++;
                else if (j > i) more++;
        }
```

```
        int medianIndex = l.size()/2;
        return less < (medianIndex +(l.size()%2))  && more <= medianIndex;
}
```

Now this solution will still produce the same median result from a list, however, it does not need as much internal storage with space complexity of only $O(1)$. Although this has come at the cost of a much slower solution with time complexity of $O(n^2)$.

9. Recursion

The Webster dictionary defines 'recurring' as: "1. To come back; to return again or repeatedly; to come again to mind. [1913 Webster]". Recursion is the act of recurring. Within computing the idea of recursion is the idea of a method calling itself. Also in computing we can have recursive data structure, these are data structures that are made up of them self. Often recursive solutions to programming problems produce much simpler code, this has many benefits in terms of producing correct and robust code. These ideas are best illustrated with some examples.

Consider the factorial function in mathematics. It is defined as:

$$n! = n*(n-1)*(n-2)*\cdots*2*1$$

If we wish to write a method that implements factorial we could use this definition and use a simple loop to create an iterative solution. This is seen below:

```
static int factorialIterative(int n) {
        int res = 1;
        for (int i=1;i<=n;i++) {
                res = res * i;
        }
        return res;
}
```

However factorial can also be defined recursively as:

$$n! = \begin{cases} n*(n-1)! & \text{if } n>0 \\ 1 & \text{if } n=0 \end{cases}$$

From this we can create a recursive solution to this problem. This produces a 'simpler' solution with no local variable and no loop. Notice how in the implementation of 'factorialRecursive' calls itself. Also notice how the implementation of 'factorialRecursive' is basically a direct translation of the recursive definition.

```
static int factorialRecursive(int n) {
        return  (n == 0 ? 1 : n * factorialRecursive(n-1));
}
```

The method works by calling itself with lower values. At some point the factorial is called with n == 0 which evaluates to 1, and hence can be returned directly. As the result is return up the stack it is multiplied by the 'n' of the particular call. This finally produces the correct result for the calling method.

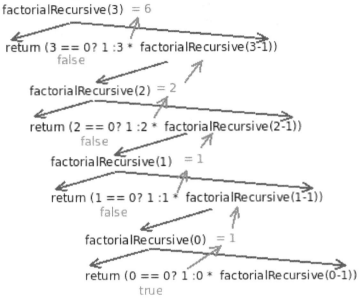

The way the recursive version of factorial works is shown in the diagram above. In some respects the workings of the recursive solution is more complex then that of the iterative approach. However, generally when developing recursive solutions you do not need to think about the details of how the method would call itself, rather, you can simply assume that a solution exists that you can make use of.

Important principles for implementing recursive solutions are:

- assume that you have a working solution to your problem that you can call,
- your solution must have a base case (or base cases) that do not involve recursive calls, and
- recursive calls must always call with parameters that are 'lesser' then those they are called from (the recursive calls must be able to work their way back to the base case(s)).

Lets take another example of a problem that we can formulate a recursive solution for. Suppose we have a full name stored in a String and we wish to extract the initials. If the name was "Eric Charles McCreath" we would like to produce the initials "ECM". Now this problem can be formulated with a recursive solution. If we take the "Eric " off the beginning of the string and extract the initial "E" then we can recursively call the method on the remaining part of the string, namely "Charles McCreath" and obtain the initials "CM". These initials can be combined giving us our final solution of "ECM". The recursive call calls itself on a shorter string, this will eventually work its way to the base case of an empty string.

```
static String initials(String name) {
        if (name.equals("")) {
                return "";
        } else {
                int spaceIndex = name.indexOf(" ");
                return name.charAt(0) +
                        initials(name.substring(spaceIndex != -1 ?
                                spaceIndex + 1: name.length())));
        }
}
```

Data structures can also be recursive. Trees and List are two simple examples of recursive data structures, these are looked at in detail in later chapters.

9.1. Additional Material

Below is an example of code used to draw this books front cover. A recursive approach is used to draw the tree.

```java
import java.awt.BasicStroke;
import java.awt.Color;
import java.awt.Dimension;
import java.awt.Font;
import java.awt.Graphics2D;
import java.awt.geom.AffineTransform;
import java.awt.geom.Line2D;
import java.awt.image.BufferedImage;
import java.io.File;
import java.io.IOException;
import java.util.Random;

import javax.imageio.ImageIO;

/*
 * Book Cover
 *
 * Eric McCreath 2010
 *
 */

public class Cover {

        static void cover(BufferedImage screen, Dimension dim) {

                Graphics2D g = screen.createGraphics();
                int xwi = (int) dim.getWidth();
                int ywi = (int) dim.getHeight();

                // draw the background
                g.setColor(Color.white);
                g.fillRect(0, 0, xwi, ywi);
                g.setColor(Color.blue);
                g.fillRect(0, (ywi/3) * 2, xwi, ywi/3);

                // draw the tree
                AffineTransform at = g.getTransform();
                g.setColor(Color.red);
                g.translate(xwi/2.0, ywi - 500.0);
```

```
                    g.scale(10.0, -10.0);
                    drawTree(g,18, new Random(0));
                    g.setTransform(at);

                    // draw the text
                    int xoff = 150;
                    int yoff = ywi/5 * 4;
                    int gap = 150;
                    g.setColor(Color.white);
                    g.setFont(new Font("Helvetica",Font.PLAIN,96));
                    g.drawString("An Introduction to Programming and" ,
                                xoff, yoff);
                    g.drawString("Software Development using Java",
                                xoff, yoff+ gap);
                    g.drawString("Eric McCreath", xoff, yoff+2*gap);
        }

        final static double treeHeight = 100.0;
        final static double angle = 0.5;
        final static double scale = 0.6;

        static void drawTree(Graphics2D g, int i, Random r) {
                g.setStroke(new BasicStroke(10.0f,BasicStroke.CAP_SQUARE,
                                        BasicStroke.JOIN_ROUND));
                g.draw(new Line2D.Double(0.0,0.0,0.0,treeHeight));
                if (i > 0) {
                        AffineTransform at = g.getTransform();
                        g.translate(0.0, treeHeight);
                        g.rotate(angle + 0.35 - ( r.nextDouble() * 0.7));
                        g.scale(scale, scale);
                        drawTree(g, i-1, r);
                        g.setTransform(at);

                        at = g.getTransform();
                        g.translate(0.0, treeHeight*0.8);
                        g.rotate(-angle + 0.35 - ( r.nextDouble() * 0.7));
                        g.scale(scale, scale);
                        drawTree(g, i-1, r);
                        g.setTransform(at);
                }
        }

        public static void main(String[] args) {
                Dimension dim = new Dimension(2270,2978);
                BufferedImage offscreen = new BufferedImage(dim.width,
                                dim.height, BufferedImage.TYPE_INT_RGB);

                cover(offscreen, dim);

                try {
                        ImageIO.write(offscreen, "png",
                                        new File("frontcoverV1.png"));
                } catch (IOException e) {
                        System.out.println("problem saving file");
                }
        }
}
```

60

10.   Implementing Lists

A List is sequence of similar elements. Generally they are index form 0. The types of operations you perform on lists include:

- **add** - add a new element to the end of the list.
- **get** - obtain an element from a particular index of the.
- **set** - overwrite an element of the list.
- **insert** - place a new element at the beginning (or a particular position) of the list.
- **iterate** - look over every element of the list.
- **size** - determine the size of the list.
- **delete** - delete elements from the list.

There are two basic ways of implementing a list. The first, and in many ways the simplest, approach is to use an array to contain the list data. The second approach is to use 'links' to connect together the elements of the list. Generally a programmer will not need to implement these, rather they will just use a standard implementation. This is what we have been doing with the ArrayList class (there is also a standard LinkedList class which we could use). However, it is very important to understand how these classes are implemented as it gives you and idea of which implementation to use given the situation in which you plan to deploy a list.

This chapter now goes through the implementation of a list of String using both approaches. In both implementations the list should act in the same way, so we have defined an interface that we expect both implementations to implement. This is defined below:

```
public interface SimpleList  {
        String get(int index);
        void set(int index, String value);
        void add(String value);  // at the end of the list
        int size();
        void insert(int index, String value);
        void delete(int index);
}
```

Although, functionally, both implementation will execute exactly the same operations with exactly the same outcomes. Their performance in terms of how long each method takes to execute and how much memory is used will be different. We briefly compare their performance at the end of this chapter, such a comparison helps programmers select the best implementation for their particular programming task.

In these implementations we have only implemented a list of String. This is to simplify the task, however, the same approach could be used for other data types or even the approach could be generalised to use `generics'.

10.1.   *Array Implementation of a List*

The array list implementation stores the strings of this list in an array. Simply elements of the list are store in corresponding elements in the array. One important distinction between arrays and lists is that lists change in size, whereas, arrays have a fixed length. To overcome this problem a size integer field is used to record the number of elements of the array that are actually in use and are part of the list.

Suppose we have a list containing the strings: "One", "Two", "Three". We may store this in an array that contains 5 elements: "One", "Two", "Three", "Junk", and "More Junk" along with the size field set to 3. So even through there is strings in the 4th and 5th elements of the array they are not part of the list given that the size of the list is 3.

Another problem that needs to be overcome when using arrays to implement lists is that as elements are added to the list the array will eventually fill up. Arrays in Java can not be extended in size. Hence, when the array fills up the implementation needs to create a new larger array and copy the old data across.

The code below shows the fields, the constructor, and the "add" and "get" methods of our implementation.

```
public class SimpleArrayList implements SimpleList {

        static final int initCapacity = 5;

        String array[];
        int size;

        public SimpleArrayList() {
                array = new String[initCapacity];
                size = 0;
        }

        public String get(int index) {
                return (String) array[index];
        }

        public void add(String value) {
                if (size == array.length)
                        addCapacity();
                array[size] = value;
                size++;
        }

        private void addCapacity() {
                String arrayBigger[] = new String[array.length * 2];
                for (int i = 0; i < size; i++) {
                        arrayBigger[i] = array[i];
                }
                array = arrayBigger;
        }
}
```

The complete implementation is available at the end of this chapter in the additional material section.

10.2. *Linked Implementation of Lists*

In the case of the linked implementation of a list, each element of the list is stored in a node and the nodes are 'linked' together. Part of such an implementation is shown below. The 'Node' class is created to store the data of each of the nodes. The 'first' field points to the Node of the list with the very first element, this Node then points to the next Node of the list which has the next element in it. The 'null' reference is used to indicate we are at the 'end' of the list. Note that in this implementation we have not checked for improper use of these methods, so if you attempted to obtain an element that is out side the bounds of the list an error would occur.

```
public class SimpleLinkedList implements SimpleList {

    Node first;

    public class Node {
        String data;
        Node next;
        public Node(String d, Node n) {
            data = d;
            next = n;
        }
    }

    public SimpleLinkedList() {
        first = null;
    }

    public void add(String value) {
        if (first == null) {
            first = new Node(value,null);
        } else {
            Node curr = first;
            while (curr.next != null) curr = curr.next;
            // curr should now be pointing at
            // the last element of the list
            curr.next = new Node(value,null);
        }
    }

    public String get(int index) {
        Node curr = first;
        for (int i =0;i<index; i++) curr = curr.next;
        return curr.data;
    }

    public int size() {
        int size = 0;
        Node curr = first;
        while (curr != null) {
            size++;
            curr = curr.next;
        }
        return size;
    }
}
```

In this implementation we only have a singly linked list. This is where the links in the list only point in one direction, in this case they point along the list in increasing index. However, it is possible to implement this class such that it points from the last element back to the first element. When programming such classes great care must be taken to get the boundary cases correct.

10.3. *Performance of Different Implementations*

The big O notation can be used to analysis the difference in performance in terms of running time. To do this we assume that n is the length of the list.

method	Array Implementation	Linked Implementation
get	O(1)	O(n)
add	O(n) *	O(n)
size	O(1)	O(n)
set	O(1)	O(n)
insert	O(n)	O(n)
delete	O(n)	O(n)

* - this is in the worst case when we need to copy the data over to a new and bigger array. Most of the time we will not need to do this. If we counted up the operations and amortised (averaged them) them over all the adds we would end up at O(1) which better reflects the cost of this operation.

From looking at a comparison of the difference in performance between the two approaches it is clear to see that the array implementation is as good as or better than that of the linked implementation. However, some minor additions to the linked implementation can greatly improve its performance. For example if a link to the last element (along with the first) was added to the implementation then the 'add' method could be done without traversing the list, hence, it would also be O(1). Another example would be you could add a field to the linked implementation class that maintained to size of the list. So when elements are added to the list it is incremented and when they are removed it is decremented. This would also mean the 'size' method would be O(1) which is the same as the array implementation.

The two implementation will also have different memory foot prints. Generally the space overhead associated with the linked implementation would be greater than that of the array representation as for each element there is the additional Node object to store. This Node object also has a pointer to the next node.

10.4. *Additional Material*

Implementation of a list of String using an array

```
public class SimpleArrayList implements SimpleList {
```

64

```
static final int initCapacity = 5;
String array[];
int size;
public SimpleArrayList() {
        array = new String[initCapacity];
        size = 0;
}

public String get(int index) {
        return (String) array[index];
}

public void add(String value) {
        if (size == array.length)
                addCapacity();
        array[size] = value;
        size++;
}

private void addCapacity() {
        String arrayBigger[] = new String[array.length * 2];
        for (int i = 0; i < size; i++) {
                arrayBigger[i] = array[i];
        }
        array = arrayBigger;
}

public void delete(int index) {
        for (int i = index; i < size - 1; i++) {
                array[i] = array[i + 1];
        }
        size--;
}


public void insert(int index, String value) {
        if (size == array.length)
                addCapacity();
        for (int i = size; i > index; i--) {
                array[i] = array[i - 1];
        }
        array[index] = value;
        size++;
}

public void set(int index, String value) {
        array[index] = value;
}

public int size() {
        return size;
}

public String toString() {
        StringBuffer sb = new StringBuffer();
        sb.append("[");
        for (int i = 0; i < size(); i++) {
                sb.append(get(i) +
                        (i < size() - 1 ? ", " : ""));
        }
```

```
            sb.append("]");
            return sb.toString();
        }
}
```

11. Implementing Trees

Trees are recursive data structures and are useful for representing information that is structured as a tree (such as mathematical expressions, content of an xml document, possible paths for a game like chess, storing tables, etc). Normally computer scientists draw trees upside down with the root of the tree at the top and the branches and leafs connecting down from the root. Formally a tree is either: a leaf node; or a inner node with one or more children (these children are also trees). In some cases the notion of an empty tree is also defined. Below is a diagram of tree with the nodes containing letters as their data:

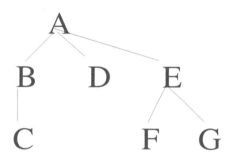

The following terminology is often used with trees:

- **nodes** – the basic components/elements that make up the tree. These would normally contain some data that is associated with the node. In some case nodes also have a index or a key. (A, B, C, D, E, F, and G are all node of the above tree)

- **root node** – this is the top (or first) node of the tree. (A in the above tree)

- **parent** – a parent node is the node from which a node directly descends. (E is the parent of F, E is the parent of G, B is the parent of C, A is the parent of B, ...)

- **children** – nodes that directly descend from a node are said to be the node's children. (B, D, and E are all the children of A)

- **leaf** – a node with no children.

- **sibling** – nodes which have the same parents are said to be siblings. (F and G are siblings)

- **inner node** – a node which has children but is not the root is said to be an inner

67

node. (B, D, and E are inner nodes)

- **size** – the size of a tree is the total number of nodes of the tree. (in this case the trees size is 7)

- **level** – the level of the root node is defined to be 1, the level of other nodes are defined to be 1 plus the level of its parent. (F has level 3)

- **height** – the height of a tree is the maximum of all the node levels. (the above tree has height 3)

- **subtrees** – the subtrees of a node are all the trees rooted at the children of that node. (The subtrees of A are the trees: B as the root node with the single child C; a tree just with leaf node D as the root; and the tree with E as the root and children E and G)

Below is some code for implementing a simple tree in which each node stores a string. This is enough to capture the information from the above example.

```java
import java.util.ArrayList;

public class GeneralTree {

    String data;
    ArrayList<GeneralTree> children;

    public GeneralTree(String d) {
        data = d;
        children = new ArrayList<GeneralTree>();
    }

    public GeneralTree addChild(GeneralTree t) {
        children.add(t);
        return this;   // By return the object we can simplify
    }                  // how a tree can be put together.

    public int size() {
        int size = 1;
        for (GeneralTree c : children) {
            size += c.size();
        }
        return size;
    }

    public int height() {
        int height = 1;
        for (GeneralTree c : children) {
            height = Math.max(height, 1 + c.height());
        }
        return height;
    }

    public String toString() {
        return "(" + data + " : " + children + ")" ;
    }
```

```
public static void main(String[] args) {
        GeneralTree gt = (new GeneralTree("A")).addChild(new
GeneralTree("B").addChild(new GeneralTree("C"))).addChild(new
GeneralTree("D")).addChild((new GeneralTree("E")).addChild(new
GeneralTree("F")).addChild(new GeneralTree("G")));  // this is the tree
                                                     // given in the
                                                     // above example
        System.out.println("size : " + gt.size());
        System.out.println("height : " + gt.height());
        System.out.println(gt);
    }
}
```

11.1. *Traversing and Searching Trees*

Often you need to be able to visit all the nodes of a tree. This is known as traversing the tree. Say you have stored an expression tree of a mathematical expression and you wish to print the expression out then you would need to traverse the tree to do this.

Also you often need to be able to find some information within a tree. Say you have stored an expression tree of a mathematical expression and you wish to find all the points in which a particular variable is used then you could search the tree to find the particular variable.   In this case you would need to traverse the entire tree to find the variables, however, in some cases the nodes of the tree would be ordered in some way in which case you can do a more targeted search.

There are two basic approaches for searching/traversing a tree:

Depth first search – this is where your search progresses down and up the tree as all nodes are visited. Such a search can be simply programmed recursively. So to traverse a tree start with the root and then recursively call depth first search on each of the children. The code for this, which could be added to the above example, is given below. Note in this code we just print the nodes as we visit them. However, we could easily modify the code to search for a particular value.

```
public void dfs() {
        System.out.println(data);
        for (GeneralTree child : children) {
                child.dfs();
        }
}
```

Breadth first search – in this approach the search goes across the tree visiting nodes of each level in tern. So the root node (level 1) is traversed first then all the nodes of level 2, then all the nodes of level 3, ... until all the levels are traversed. Coding this search is a little more involved than that of the depth first approach. Generally a que is used to store and order which nodes need to be searched next.   This has a memory overhead associated with it which can cripple a program if the tree is large enough.   The code for such a breadth first

69

search is given below:

```
public void bfs() {
    LinkedList<GeneralTree> que = new LinkedList<GeneralTree>();
    que.add(this);
    while(que.size() > 0) {
        GeneralTree curr = que.remove();
                    // take the first element in the que
        System.out.println(curr.data);
        que.addAll(curr.children);
                    // add children to the end of the que
    }
}
```

Another approach that can be used is to create a loop which does each level in tern (use an index which goes from 1 to the height of the tree). And then for each level use a depth first approach to find all the node of a that particular level. Note this does not have the memory overhead of the above approach, however, it ends up traversing the nodes many more times.

Note in some cases the tree is never explicitly stored, rather, parts of the tree are constructed when required. For example if you are writing a program which needed to search a very large tree of possibilities (such as the Chess game tree or the tree of possible configurations for designing an electronic circuit) you would never store the entire tree, rather, you would just work out the nodes as you needed them. Generally you would only need to store the path from the root of the tree to the current node you are exploring.

Some trees may also be infinite (or very very large) in size. Clearly these trees can not be explicitly stored in a computer, however, they may be represented and parts of them may be searched or traversed. The Chess game tree is a good example of a very very large tree[3] which could not be stored or even entirely explored in a modern computer. However, it is possible to search part of the tree thus creating a very good Chess playing machine. When trees are infinite or very large care must be taken when selecting the searching approach, often a breadth first approach is used rather than a depth first as the depth first approach will often get caught descending ever deeper down one branch of the tree.

11.2. *Binary Search Trees*

A binary tree is a tree in which each node has at most 2 children. The children of each node are generally labelled the 'left' child or the 'right' child. These trees occur in a number of situations (simple mathematical expressions are generally binary trees). Also they can be used to store sorted information in which entries of a particular key can be quickly retrieved. Such trees can store a table and are known as binary search trees. Binary search trees are the focus of this section. Formally binary search trees have a 'key' for each node and are recursively defined as follows:

---

3   Note that, the tree of Chess states is not infinite because of the Chess rule that calls a draw after enough repetitions of the same position.

1. all the nodes to the left of the root have key values which are less than the root's key value,

2. all the nodes to the right of the root have key values which are greater than the root's key value,

3. the left sub-tree is a binary search tree, and

4. the right sub-tree is a binary search tree.

Nodes of a particular tree can be looked up without traversing the entire tree. A path from the root to the node you are searching for can be simply found by comparing the current key with that of the key you are searching for. If the key is the same then you have found the required node, if the key you are searching for is less than that of the current key then traverse to the left, if greater traverse to the right. Note also if there is no child in the direction you wish to traverse then that key is not in the tree.

The example code of a binary search tree is given below. This code implements a table for looking up strings using an integer as the key.

```java
public interface Table {
    public String get(int key);
    public Table put(int key, String data);
}
public class BinTree implements Table {
    int key;
    String data;
    Table left, right;

    public BinTree(int key, String data, Table left, Table right) {
        this.key = key;
        this.data = data;
        this.left = left;
        this.right = right;
    }

    public String get(int k) {
            if (k == key) {
            return data;
            } else if (k < key) {
            return left.get(k);
        } else {
            return right.get(k);
        }
    }

    public Table put(int k, String d) {
        if (k == key) {
            return new BinTree(k,d,left,right);
        } else if (k < key) {
            return new BinTree(key,data,left.put(k, d), right);
        } else {
            return new BinTree(key,data,left, right.put(k, d));
        }
```

```
        }
}

public class EmptyBinTree implements Table {
      public String get(int key) {
              return null;
      }

      public Table put(int k, String d) {
              return new BinTree(k,d, new EmptyBinTree(), this);
      }
}
```

12.   Implementing Hash Tables

A hash table (or hash map) provides a very efficient way of storing table type information.   In a table you look up entries using a key. If a simple array (or linked list) is used for a table then when a value is looked up each entry needs to be search until the correct one is found. This is an $O(n)$ operation where n is the number of elements in the table.   If a sorted binary tree is used then this lookup operation is reduced to $O(lg\ n)$ (this assumes the binary tree is balanced).   Now if a hash table is used lookups can be done in O(1) time (this assumes the hashing function is 'random' for the keys being added - this is generally the case).

This chapter presents the basic idea behind how these classes are implemented. Once again a programmer would generally not implement such a class they would just use a standard implementation, such as HashMap in Java, however, it is useful to understand how such classes work so that you can best apply them in a given situation.

The main two methods of a hash table are:

- **put** - adds a new entry with a particular key (if the table already contains an entry with the same key then normally the old entry is replace with the new), and

- **get** - this looks up the table and returns the data for a particular key.

Implementations will also often provide:

- **remove** - delete an entry from the table,

- **size** - determine the number of entries in the table, and

- **keys** - return, as a list, all the keys in the table (this is useful if you wish to traverse all the entries of the table).

In our example implementation we create a table that uses a string as the key and a double as the value to look up. The interface for this table is:

```
public interface Table {
    public Double get(String key);
    public Table put(String key, Double data);
    public Table remove(String key);
    public Integer size();
}
```

The hash table is stored within an array. Each entry in the array is called a 'bucket'. As we wish to look up an entry quickly we can not afford to search through all the entries to find correct bucket, rather, we use a 'hashing function' to help find the bucket the entry is stored in.   The hashing function basically takes the key and turns it into an integer.   The hash function must always map the same key to the same integer. In this simple hash table implementation the hashing function is calculated by summing the character values of the string[4].

```
static int hash(String key) {
    int res = 0;
    for (int i = 0; i < key.length(); i++) {
        res += (int) key.charAt(i);
    }
    return res;
}
```

This function would map the key "Eric" to 387. Now as these numbers are mostly much bigger than the number of buckets we have, so we modulo this number by the size of the bucket array. Say our hash table has 4 buckets then 387 % 4 = 3. So, all going well, the entry for "Eric" would be located at bucket 3 in our array of buckets. Most of the time when we either add an entry or lookup an entry we use this simple approach to find the correct bucket from the key. However, there may also be other keys that map to the same bucket! So the entry for "Jill" would also map to bucket 395 % 4 = 3. This is known as a collision. The implementation addresses the collision problem by storing the key along side the data which enables a check to take place. In addition to this check the hash implementation will normally use one of two approaches:

- **linear probing** – in this approach when a collision occurs the entry is added (or can be found) in the next available space. So in the above example if "Eric" was the only entry in the table (in bucket 3) and we added "Jill" (also indexing to bucket 3) then a collision would occur so "Jill" would be put into the next available buck, in this case it would wrap around and be put into bucket 0. Also if "Jill" was looked up in the table then the hash function along with the modulo would direct the lookup to bucket 3 which would be the location of "Eric", because of a possible collision the bucket would be checked for "Jill" this is done until either "Jill" or an empty bucket is found.

- **chaining** – in this approach each bucket stores a list (normally using a linked list) of entries. So new entries would just get added to the list, also when searching is done the list needs to be traversed to find the key.

The diagram below shows the table for the discussed example. Also shown is the hashing function and the data structures for the linear probing and chaining approaches.

---

4   Generally more effort is put into creating these functions such that integer values are better spread out. Also there may be some problems with this implementation when strings get very long. This is because the integer addition may overflow.

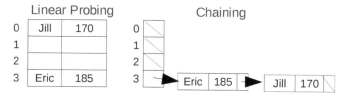

The Table

Key	Data
Eric	185
Jill	170

Hashing function

hash(Eric) → 387 % 4 → 3
hash(Jill) → 395 % 4 → 3

Linear Probing

0	Jill	170
1		
2		
3	Eric	185

Chaining

At some point the number of buckets will not be enough for the number of elements in the table.   The ratio of the number of elements in the table to the number of actual buckets is known as the load factor.   Generally when the load factor is pushed over a certain thresh-hold a new larger array of buckets is created and all the entries are copied over (bucket locations need to be recalculated for every entry).   The load factor would often be set at about 0.7 as anything over this starts to produce a great deal of collisions reducing the hash table's performance.

The code for the linear probing approach is given below:

```
public class HashTable implements Table {
    static final Integer startBuckets = 4;
                                // normally this would be bigger
    static final Double load = 0.7;

    public class Entry {
        String key;
        Double data;
        public Entry(String k, Double d) {
            key = k;
            data = d;
        }
    }

    Integer size;
    Entry buckets[];

    public HashTable() {
        buckets = new Entry[startBuckets];
        for (int i = 0; i < buckets.length; i++) {
            buckets[i] = null;
        }
        size = 0;
    }

    static public Integer hash(String k) {
                    // this returns a non-negative integer.
        Integer res = 0;
        for (int i = 0; i < k.length(); i++) {
            res +=   (int) k.charAt(i);
        }
        return res;
```

```
        }

        public Double get(String k) {
                Integer index = hash(k) % buckets.length;
                Integer pos = index;
                do {
                        if (buckets[pos] == null)
                                return null;
                        if (buckets[pos].key.equals(k))
                                return buckets[pos].data;
                        pos = (pos + 1) % buckets.length;
                } while (pos != index);
                return null;
        }

        public Table put(String k, Double d) {
                if (size >= load * buckets.length)
                        increasesize();
                Integer index = hash(k) % buckets.length;
                Integer pos = index;
                do {
                        if (buckets[pos] == null) {
                                buckets[pos] = new Entry(k, d);
                                size++;
                                return this;
                        }
                        if (buckets[pos].key.equals(k)) {
                                buckets[pos].data = d;
                                return this;
                        }
                        pos = (pos + 1) % buckets.length;
                } while (pos != index);
                return null;
        }

        private void increasesize() {
                Entry oldbuckets[] = buckets;
                buckets = new Entry[2*oldbuckets.length];
                size = 0;
                for (int i = 0; i < oldbuckets.length; i++) {
                        if (oldbuckets[i] != null) {
                                String k = oldbuckets[i].key;
                                Double d = oldbuckets[i].data;
                                put(k,d);
                        }
                }
        }
}
```

These tables can be traversed by traversing the buckets and noting the non-empty locations. The order in which you put elements into the table will generally not be the same as the order in which the table is traversed.

Removing entries from the table with the chaining approach is simple just lookup the bucket for the given key, traverse the chain, and delete the entry when found. However, removing entries when linear probing is used is considerable more complex, as empting one bucket may also involve shifting other buckets to maintain the integrity of the data structure.

13.   Concurrency

Modern computers normally have many activities all going on at once. So for example as I type this sentence my: email client is running, I have a small clock running at the bottom of my window, there is an application which tells me the weather in Canberra, a programming is running to keep the windows displayed, etc. Overall there is 230 programs running on my desktop!   The CPU I have is 'dual core' so at any one point in time there is at most 2 programs actually running on my computer. The operating system rapidly switches the 230 running programs on the 2 cores giving the appearance of them all running at the same time.

A 'process' is a program in execution. Processes can be made up of one or more threads. Threads are the entities which execute the code sequentially in your program. Any method you implement in a program will be 'realised' via a thread going through it step by step, going around the loops, changing the values of variables due to an assignments, etc..   The threads of a process share global data so changes of data in one thread are 'seen' by other threads of that process.

When writing a program generally you will do it with just a single thread executing the code. However, in some cases it is useful to have more than one thread executing at the same time on your code. This could be because it simplifies the structure of your code as there are 'concurrent' activities taking place. For example a web server program will be generally dealing with a number of web requests at the same time. By attaching each request to its own thread simplifies the coding of the server, as each thread is able to keep track of the state of a single web request.   Or in some cases you may have a large amount of computation to do, so by getting a number of threads each to do part of the computation you are able to improve the performance of the program.

13.1.   Java Threads

In Java the 'Thread' class provides a simple way of creating concurrent threads of execution. When constructing a Thread you provide it with an object which implements the Runnable interface.   Classes that implement the Runnable interface have a 'run' method. This 'run' method is executed when the thread is started. Threads can be started via the 'start' method. Note after the start method is executed you can imaging another thread of execution running along side the thread that started it. This is depicted below with time running down the page and a new thread of execution starting in the right column.

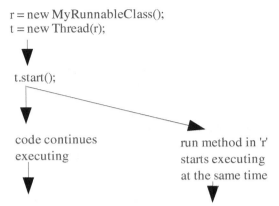

```
r = new MyRunnableClass();
t = new Thread(r);
```

t.start();

code continues
executing

run method in 'r'
starts executing
at the same time

The below example creates two new threads, one with the name 'A' and the other with the name 'B'. The threads just loop around saying their names. The thread that started the two threads stops until threads 'A' and 'B' finish (this is done with the 'join' method).

```java
import java.util.Random;
public class MyRunner implements Runnable {
        static Random rand = new Random();

        String name;
        public MyRunner(String n) {
                name = n;
        }
        public void run() {
                for (int i = 0; i < 4; i++) {
                        System.out.println("running : " + name );
                        try {
                                Thread.sleep(rand.nextInt(100));
                        } catch (InterruptedException e) {
                        }
                }
        }
}
public class ThreadExample  {
        public static void main(String[] args) throws InterruptedException
{
                MyRunner arunner = new MyRunner("A");
                MyRunner brunner = new MyRunner("B");
                Thread athread = new Thread(arunner);
                Thread bthread = new Thread(brunner);
                athread.start(); // start the threads running
                bthread.start();
                athread.join();  // The join method will stop
                                 // this main thread
                bthread.join();  // executing until the referenced
                                 // thread completes.
        }
}
```

13.2. Race Conditions

The introduction of more than one thread into your program which are making changes to the program's data introduces an enormous amount of complexity. The possibility of one thread interacting with another thread in an unexpected way becomes high. A number of threads may depend on a shared state. When this shared state is updated serially by the threads the program may work 100% correctly. This correctness may also be independent of the order in which the threads execute their code. However, when their execution is interleaved, there may be an error in the final state. This is known as a race condition.

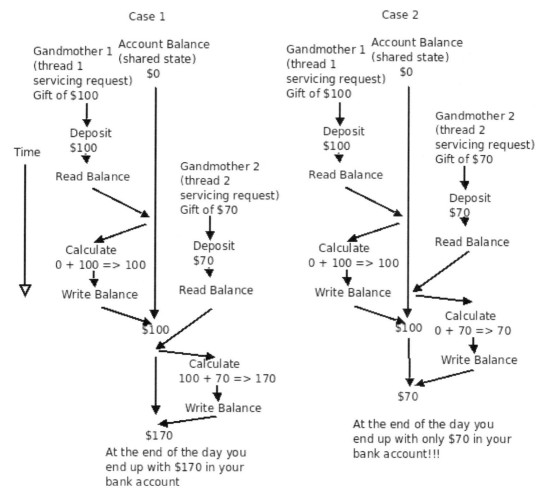

Example of race condition when money is deposited into a bank account.

An example, as depicted in the Figure above, of a race condition is now given. Suppose we have a banking program. Basically the banking program maintains the balance of your bank account. The types of requests on this data would include deposit money, withdraw money, obtain the current balance, etc. Now for efficiency reasons each request could be achieved by a single new thread, this would enable the banking server to service many request at the same time. Now suppose it is your birthday and you get $100 from one grandmother and $70 from your other grandmother. Assuming you had no money in your account at the beginning of the day then at the end of the day you should have $170 in your account (shown in case 1 of the Figure). However if you are very unfortunate and the depositing threads overlap in time you may end up with either only $70 or only $100 at the end of the day! This is shown in case 2 of the Figure.

Great care must be taken to avoid these situations when you have a number of threads all operating on some shared data. The operations on these shared states are called `critical sections'. Generally, a programmer will attempt to make them 'atomic'. This is where the outcome of the concurrent execution is as if it was executed one after the other (in any order). Locks provide one way of making critical sections atomic. So in the bank account example a lock could be associated with the account balance and any thread wishing to deposit money must first obtain this lock then do the deposit and then release the lock. Hence if another thread came along and wished to deposit money at the same time that the initial thread is in the critical section (and hence has the lock) this new thread would just wait for the initial thread to complete and release the lock.

14. References and Resources

- The Java™ Language Specification, Third Edition, James Gosling, Bill Joy, Guy Steele, Gilad Bracha, ADDISON-WESLEY, Came be downloaded from external link: http://java.sun.com/docs/books/jls/ This book provides a details description of the Java language. It is very much a reference book.

- Java SE 6 API. external link: http://java.sun.com/javase/6/docs/api/ Also this is on the local file system in the CSIT labs at : file:///usr/share/doc/sun-java6-jdk/html/index.html

- Cay Horstmann's Big Java textbook web site. external link: http://www.horstmann.com/bigjava.html

- Sun's Java Tutorials. external link: http://java.sun.com/docs/books/tutorial/index.html

15. Appendix

15.1. Forest Fire Example Simulation

This is a simple 2D simulation of a forest fire written in Java. Trees burn which let out embers, these are blown by some wind and they then set other trees burning. A screen shot during a simulation is shown below:

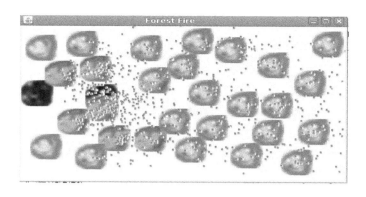

The UML class diagram for this is shown below:

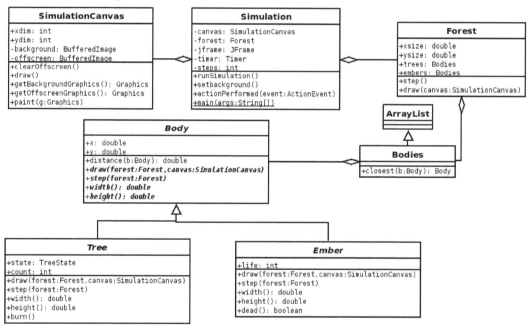

The code is also available in :
http://cs.anu.edu.au/student/comp1110.2010/Simulation.jar

To run the simulation from the command line execute:

```
| % java -jar Simulation.jar
```

To unpack and examine the code you can from the command line execute:

```
| % jar xf Simulation.jar
```

It is worth doing this from within an empty directory.